MALCOLM X
AT OXFORD UNION

TRANSGRESSING BOUNDARIES

Studies in Black Politics and Black Communities

Cathy Cohen and Fredrick Harris, Series Editors

Malcolm X at Oxford Union

Racial Politics in a Global Era

Saladin Ambar

OXFORD
UNIVERSITY PRESS

OXFORD

UNIVERSITY PRESS

Oxford University Press is a department of the University of Oxford.
It furthers the University's objective of excellence in research, scholarship,
and education by publishing worldwide.

Oxford   New York

Auckland   Cape Town   Dar es Salaam   Hong Kong   Karachi
Kuala Lumpur   Madrid   Melbourne   Mexico City   Nairobi
New Delhi   Shanghai   Taipei   Toronto

With offices in

Argentina   Austria   Brazil   Chile   Czech Republic   France   Greece
Guatemala   Hungary   Italy   Japan   Poland   Portugal   Singapore
South Korea   Switzerland   Thailand   Turkey   Ukraine   Vietnam

Oxford is a registered trademark of Oxford University Press
in the UK and certain other countries.

Published in the United States of America by
Oxford University Press
198 Madison Avenue, New York, NY 10016

Library of Congress Cataloging-in-Publication Data
Ambar, Saladin M.
Malcolm X at Oxford Union : racial politics in a global era / by Saladin Ambar.
pages cm.
ISBN 978-0-19-997547-1 (hardback)   1. X, Malcolm, 1925–1965—Political and social
views.   2. Speeches, addresses, etc., American.   3. Oxford Union.   4. Debates and
debating—England.   5. African Americans—Politics and government.   6. United States—Politics and
government—1963-1969.   7. African Americans—Civil rights.   8. Blacks—Politics and government.   9. Blacks—Civil rights.   10. Human rights.   11. Civil rights.   I. Title.
BP223.Z8L57163 2014
320.54'6092—dc23
2013026072

1 3 5 7 9 8 6 4 2
Printed in the United States of America
on acid-free paper

In Memory of
Ralph Lamb and for his grandchildren
Gabby, Luke, and Daniel

You are certainly right when you say that this is only part of a world-wide problem.

—President Lyndon B. Johnson,
private telegram to British Prime Minister
Harold Wilson, 1965

CONTENTS

CHRONOLOGY OF KEY EVENTS

1959 May: Murder of Kelso Cochrane in London, less than one year after the Notting Hill Riots.

July: Malcolm X travels to Egypt, Mecca, Iran, Syria, and Ghana as representative of Elijah Muhammad.

1960 June: Congo gains independence; beginning of "Congo Crisis." Nearly 20 African nations gain their independence in 1960.

September: Malcolm X meets with Fidel Castro in Harlem.

Fourteen African states gain independence from France.

1961 February: Malcolm X leads demonstration at the UN protesting the assassination of the Congo's Prime Minister Patrice Lumumba.

October: Paris witnesses terror campaign against Algerians; upwards of 200 Algerians are murdered by Paris police forces.

1962 April: Commonwealth Immigrants Act passed in UK.

Shooting of Nation of Islam member Ronald Stokes in Los Angeles.

1963 August: March on Washington, DC; Paris march on US Embassy.

November: Malcolm X delivers "Message to the Grass Roots" speech.

Malcolm X calls the assassination of President Kennedy a case of "chickens coming home to roost."

December: Malcolm X is suspended for ninety days for remarks about President Kennedy.

Kenya gains independence from Great Britain.

1964   February: Lord Plowden Report released, detailing diplomatic impact of end of British Empire.

March: Malcolm X announces his departure from Nation of Islam and the formation of the Muslim Mosque, Incorporated (MMI).

Conservative Party candidate Peter Griffiths (UK) refuses to disavow racist campaign slogan in Smethwick, England.

April: Malcolm X delivers "Ballot or the Bullet" speech; makes pilgrimage to Mecca.

May: Malcolm X travels to Nigeria, Ghana, and other African states.

June: Malcolm X announces the formation of the Organization of Afro-American Unity (OAAU); meets with Japanese *Hibakushas*.

July: Malcolm X observes filibuster of civil rights bill in US Senate; visits Cairo, Egypt.

Algeria gains independence from France.

Barry Goldwater delivers remarks at Republican National Convention.

August: Philadelphia riots erupt.

September: Malcolm X travels to Africa, meets with 11 heads of state by mid-October.

October: Great Britain elects Labour Party candidate Harold Wilson prime minister over Conservative Party candidate Alec Douglas-Home.

China explodes an atomic bomb, becoming the world's fifth nuclear power.

November: Malcolm X speaks in Paris, France; accepts invitation to speak at Oxford.

President Lyndon B. Johnson is reelected over Republican challenger Senator Barry M. Goldwater.

December: Malcolm X speaks at Oxford Union debate, visits Manchester, Sheffield, UK.

1965   January: Malcolm X interviews with leaders of Young Socialist Alliance (YSA).

February: Malcolm X visits London, Smethwick, England; he is denied entry to France. He is assassinated on February 21 in Harlem.

August: Watts rebellion erupts in California.

December: Great Britain passes first Race Relations Act.

A NOTE FROM THE AUTHOR

I have chosen to keep the spelling and punctuation from original texts and sources used in this book. In an effort to avoid awkwardness and confusion, I have also elected to employ "Malcolm" throughout the text in lieu of "X," as the Nation of Islam's membership consisted of innumerable "Xs." I beg the reader's indulgence for any presumed familiarity.

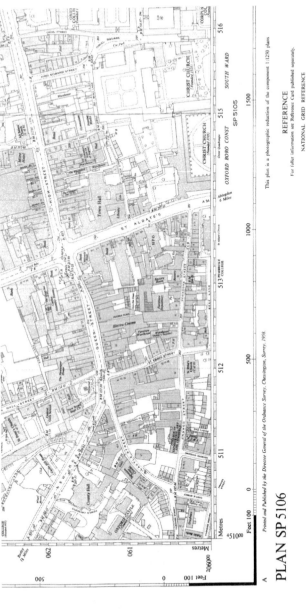

Map of Oxford area, 1958
Bodleian Library, Oxford University

Prologue: 1964

The fall of 1964 was a season of political contrasts in America. The Civil Rights Act that passed that summer—a real one, far superior to its 1957 and 1960 progenitors—led many Americans to believe liberalism was on the ascent. Dr. Martin Luther King Jr.'s Nobel Peace Prize, awarded in October, offered further proof to the world that racial strife in America was eroding—that the democratic ideals of Thomas Jefferson were close to being realized. In November, President Lyndon Baines Johnson was reelected, defeating Arizona Senator Barry Goldwater by an overwhelming margin. Racial progress in America, however "deliberate," continued to be portrayed as evidence of capitalism and democracy's superiority over the surprisingly stubborn march of global communism. Reason was conquering extremism. The riots in Harlem and Philadelphia earlier in the year were worrisome, to be sure, but they were more reflective of the nation's past than its future. A year after President Kennedy's assassination, Camelot may have been dead, but the sense that the United States could do great and powerful things abided. A Great Society was close at hand. And yet, as always is the case, the nation's residual unease, the underlying dark truths it sought to cloak, had its share of spokesmen. There was no other person in the United States who punctured this image of racial and national progress more than Malcolm X. What America sought to forget, Malcolm hoped to memorialize.

Having left the Nation of Islam in March of 1964, Malcolm made his historic pilgrimage to Mecca in April, and in short order, completed other memorable and extensive trips to Africa and the

Middle East. What Americans know of Malcolm X as an international figure has mostly to do with these travels. What is less known is that Malcolm X had strong interests in delivering his message to Europe as well, and that he spent significant time in both France and the United Kingdom shortly before his assassination. Malcolm was also interested in expanding the list of nations in Western Europe he hoped to visit, states where he would advocate on the behalf of the still-marginalized black population in the United States. His ultimate objective was to bring their case before the world at the United Nations. But first he had to build support. So in late 1964, Malcolm became a man in exile—in part escaping the threat of assassination at home, while simultaneously seeking to build a diasporic coalition of black, Asian, and Muslim support in Western capitals such as Paris and London. By late November, an invitation arrived in his Harlem office. It was an offer to speak at Oxford University as part of the Oxford Union Society's end-of-semester debate. The topic for debate was chosen from Barry Goldwater's already famous line delivered during his acceptance speech at the Republican National Convention: "Extremism in the defense of liberty is no vice. Moderation in the pursuit of justice is no virtue."

Malcolm accepted the invitation, and would soon hurl himself into the world of 1964 British politics. That October, Labour's Harold Wilson had defeated the Conservative Alec Douglas-Home by a narrow margin. The industrial city of Smethwick, in the Midlands area of Great Britain, just outside of Birmingham, had become the center of attention early on, as the issues of immigration and race conjoined in ways that called into question the very notion of "Englishness." Malcolm's visit to Oxford and subsequent visit to Smethwick—where black and South Asian immigrants faced acute housing discrimination—served to call attention to the ways in which people of color were in varying states of revolt not only in their former colonial homes, but also within the centers of Western nations themselves. It was the master's house that was now threatened.

At Oxford, Malcolm X delivered one of the truly great addresses of the civil rights movement. It remains a lost rhetorical jewel from that era. Perhaps more important, Malcolm's speech at Oxford owes its significance not so much to the revelatory power of its words, but for what it revealed about its time—and indeed our own. The Oxford moment speaks to a time when race, immigration, decolonization, international politics, and the nature of power in the world were all in a state of flux. And it was Malcolm X, not solely as an American, but also as an international figure, who best spoke to this moment. No other speech of Malcolm's captures his political thought's complexity, development, and potential global reach as well as Oxford. And no other speech of his challenges our present political ethos as well with respect to both issues of race and the nation's foreign policy. It is the purpose of this book to uncover this moment and help put it in a context that can help better explain our own time—one in which America's relationship with both domestic and international forces of racial, ethnic, religious, and economic change is in rapid transition. The same can be said for America's Western allies—especially France and Great Britain. Malcolm at Oxford is thus a moment that speaks to us best when we recognize the ongoing and interrelated struggle between ideas of national identity and the lure of political domination at home and abroad.

Perhaps the venue of Oxford highlighted the prosecutorial and didactic fervor that undergirded Malcolm's rhetorical style. It is a speech difficult to classify; it is neither nationalistic nor *postracial*. It neither rejects nor genuflects before the altar of Western intellectual traditions. It is at once the speech of a Muslim, a secularist, a humanist, and a black revolutionary. It is both pragmatic in its opening analysis and idealistic in its denouement. It is also so deeply American, it might be said to be *liberal*. In thirty short minutes Malcolm X stands before a diverse and largely sympathetic audience at Oxford—and takes the topic of extremism through the thought milieu of his time—the crisis of the newly independent Congo and America's involvement in the aerial bombardment of that nation's black civilians; the racial politics involved in enforcing the Civil Rights Act; the role of the media in shaping racially contingent perceptions of right and wrong; and lastly, the right of any people to "take up arms against a sea of troubles and by opposing end them."

It would seem that we are far removed from the Oxford Moment today. The United States has not reelected a Southerner named Johnson, but a Chicagoan named Obama. Liberalism once again seems ascendant. The calls for a postracial America have never been louder. And, the nation seems poised to enter into a demographic dreamscape of educated white progressives, Latinos, African Americans, Asians, women, and lower-income workers of every stripe, banding together as a winning coalition well into the twenty-first century. Perhaps the Oxford speech's obscurity is more well-deserved now than ever before. And yet, we can hear Malcolm call out to the nation from Oxford, condemning its use of predator drone strikes, as we hear his critique of an American-financed air campaign in the Congo. We can hear his deconstruction of the racialized politics of Congress in 1964 even now, in a nation still devoid of a single elected black senator, with black unemployment still nearly twice that of whites, and with a party system that has virtually no place for public discourse about poverty. And in the fiery *banlieues* of Paris, suburbs of London, and capitals of North Africa, we can hear Malcolm's Oxford warning for our generation of unrest—if we are willing to listen.

"In my opinion, the young generation of whites, blacks, browns, whatever else there is, you're living at a time of extremism, a time of revolution, a time when there's got to be a change," Malcolm implored. "People in power have misused it, and now there has to be a change." Malcolm's closing argument at Oxford was an appeal that defied racial, religious, and class identities. It was largely a plea to the youth, whom Malcolm believed held the only possible key to saving a world not on the precipice of unimagined prosperity and renewal, but rather on the brink of deepened chaos and despair. Malcolm's critique at Oxford cannot be mistaken for an embrace of this grim possibility. It was, arguably, one of the best defenses—extreme though it might have been—for a radical departure from it. As millions of people around the world heard Malcolm X for the first time at Oxford—a byproduct of the BBC's exclusive television broadcast—it is worth considering how we may be truly hearing him for the first time today, by going back to those 30 minutes in an anxious debate hall, some 50 years ago.

Chapter 1

Introduction: "This is an interesting despatch"

Malcolm X walked though the swinging doors of the Oxford Union debate hall to warm applause. The left and right doors were marked "Noes" and "Ayes," respectively. Their ancient purpose was for the registering of votes. Since 1823, the Oxford Union Society had been holding such debates, and the doors bore the hallmarks of tradition in their function and signage.[1] In 1964, the Union debate topics ranged from the forgettable to the sublime. "This House prefers the Beatles to Beethoven" was the subject for debate just five weeks prior to Malcolm's visit. On this occasion, however, the motion was "Extremism in the defence of Liberty is no vice; moderation in the pursuit of Justice is no virtue." Malcolm took the affirmative.

Taller and leaner than his colleagues entering the hall that evening, Malcolm sought his seat briskly, unsmiling. He had politely eschewed the wearing of tails, as had been customary for speakers at the Union, wearing instead his familiar black suit and narrow straight tie.[2] As he maneuvered to his seat across the wooden floor and parliamentary trappings of the hall, Malcolm took in the applause and began his preparations for what would amount to his last full speech before an international audience. Broadcast that evening by the BBC, the debate provided perhaps the only time the world would take in Malcolm X beyond mere sound bites.

The British government was not so uninformed. Malcolm was a well-known quantity to the British Foreign Office, and his political insights and objectives had been closely followed by UK authorities for some time. Well over a year before his trip to Oxford, the British

Embassy in Washington saw him as a "better known, younger, sharper, more modern figure" than the Nation of Islam's leader, Elijah Muhammad. "[He] gives an impression," wrote Dennis A. Greenhill in his lengthy dispatch about black organizations in the United States, "of being able to use his power to good political effect."[3] Greenhill's 52-page report highlighted the potential turn toward militancy in the American civil rights movement. In reporting on his meeting with President John F. Kennedy's special assistant for civil rights matters, Lee White, Greenhill indirectly illuminated the key to Malcolm's popularity among blacks at home, and his penchant for stoking concern among European governments abroad:

> Mr. White stressed the significance of the rivalries among the various Negro leaders which had been becoming very obvious. He suspected that several of the Negro leaders would have preferred to avoid demonstrations while Congress was considering the pending [Civil Rights Act] legislation. But it was clear that no Negro leader could afford to recommend this for fear of losing his following. The pressure away from moderation produced by this contest for leadership was very real.[4]

For years as the spokesman for the Honorable Elijah Muhammad, Malcolm had been castigating, and at times ridiculing, Martin Luther King Jr. and other civil rights leaders for what he deemed to be their overly moderate stance. Interestingly, by the time of his visit to Oxford, Malcolm would be mailing form letters to those same leaders and organizations, informing them of his changed worldview and requesting to meet. While Malcolm would ultimately come to see the radical purpose behind direct nonviolent confrontation, he also remained a perennial thorn in the side of white indifference to racial injustice. As Greenhill noted in his report, "The Black Muslims are there, ready to exploit failure."[5] In no uncertain terms, this was the central role Malcolm played in his pas de deux with the US government. It was a role of clear importance to London as well as Washington. Beyond assessing the ugliness of Birmingham, Alabama, in the spring of 1963, the British government was evaluating the empirical data that seemed to all but forecast a full-scale Negro revolution. Greenhill's report noted that only 6.2 percent of voting age blacks in Mississippi could vote in 1963; in Georgia, only 15 percent were even registered. In Texas, only 2.6 percent of black students attended desegregated schools. This paltry figure represented the greatest percentage in the Deep South.

The situation was so appalling that Prime Minster Harold Macmillan weighed in on Greenhill's dispatch, commenting in his own hand on a separate Foreign Office document: "This is an interesting despatch. The figures in paragraph 5 are remarkable. H.M." In what appears to be a bit of an afterthought, Macmillan offers the type of colonial connection to American racial injustice that Malcolm would feature so powerfully at Oxford: "How can the U.S. really support the extending of the franchise in S-Rhodesia? H."[6] It is clear that Greenhill's Dispatch 116 had become a bit of a cause célèbre in the inner circles of the British Foreign Office. This was the case even while it was being pieced together. Greenhill preempted his own report in an effort to allay fears at home that the volatility of American race relations might be so significant as to alter British foreign policy. Writing one month before the March on Washington, Greenhill was cautiously optimistic:

Dear Bernard,
Thank you for your letter of July 26 about the Chief of Defence Staff's enquiry on Civil Rights and internal security here.

We are in fact nearing completion of a Despatch on this subject, but on looking at the Draft I find that was one aspect which, as you thought, we had not covered. The reason was that our analysts had led us to the conclusion that there was no significant threat to internal security at the present time—certainly not of such a degree as to affect United States defence commitments overseas.[7]

Underlying Malcolm's visit to the UK in late 1964, and his return in early 1965, was the sensitivity among British officials to the links between the American civil rights movement, British foreign policy, and the objectives of empire, waning as they were. No other American personality reflected this tripartite nature of American race relations as well as Malcolm. When Martin Luther King began speaking out against the "evil triplets" of racism, militarism, and materialism in American society in 1967, he was in many respects articulating a message honed by Malcolm over many years.[8] The possibility of black insurrection in the United States drew British officials to a set of circumstances they were most familiar with—colonial rule. Reflecting on the findings of Dispatch 116, the British ambassador to the United States, Patrick Henry Dean, concluded after the Watts rebellion in 1965:

It is difficult not to draw a certain parallel with developments in the colonial field of Africa, whereby moderate African leaders who were able to negotiate sensibly staged constitutional advances with Colonial Governments were continually outbid by more extreme nationalist leaders. The colonial regimes were thus compelled eventually to use force to contain the extremists up to a certain point, but could ultimately only resolve the problem with the grant of outright independence. Since the solution is not possible for the Negroes in the United States (and I do not imagine that the Black Muslim demand for some sort of separate black area can ever be really remotely practicable) it seems clear that the Negro extremists here, whether or not their aims be political or blatantly criminal, will also have to be dealt with by *an increasing and perhaps indefinitely continued use of force.*[9]

As we will see, Malcolm's extensive analysis of the situation in the Congo in 1964 at Oxford was strategic to his thinking about racial justice in a global context. This perspective emphasized going beyond the nation's capital in Washington to others at the heart of the colonial enterprise as well—namely London and Paris. In this regard, Malcolm's understanding of the complexity of racial injustice as a global phenomenon was more in tune with British policymakers' views than those in the United States. Naturally, Malcolm would have been somewhat pleased to know that the British prime minister shared his view of American democracy's inherent hypocrisy. And, undoubtedly, he would have felt affirmed by Ambassador Dean's harsh calculus of America's political will to deal with the "extremists" in the country's midst by employing the use of force "indefinitely." For those audience members in attendance at Oxford—many of whom were of African and Asian descent—Malcolm's presence was not primarily about his stature as a fighter for American racial justice, or even that of an extremist. He represented, as much as anything at Oxford, a bridge between the seemingly divided movements for American civil rights and independence from colonial rule. The cast of characters at Oxford on the evening of December 3, 1964—and the speech itself—would in time come to reflect the same unity of purpose.

The Oxford Union of 1964

The Oxfordshire Record Office has among its collection of interesting documents an old black-and-white photograph featuring the participants in the 1964 Oxford Union Society debate (see figure 1.1).[10] There, in the austere-looking library, sits Malcolm X, on the bottom row, just right of center. His hands clasped in his lap, but with the faint hint of a smile, Malcolm appears as do so many of the scores of men and women whose faces have adorned the walls surrounding the anteroom of the debating chamber; he is formal and impassive in rigidity. The sense of uniformity one gets from viewing these photographs dating back over nearly a hundred years of debates is almost numbing. And yet the 1964 photograph is striking for the inherent iconoclasm of its subjects. Malcolm X—"the Black Muslim come to Oxford" as he was described by the *Oxford Mail*—was but one of the individuals present at Oxford that day whose presence foretold of the

FIGURE 1.1 Official photo, December 3, 1964, Oxford Union debate. (Gillman & Soame)

way Oxford, the United Kingdom, and indeed, much of the Western world, was changing.[11]

To Malcolm's right was seated the society's president, Eric Anthony Abrahams of St. Peter's College (see figure 1.2). Unlike Malcolm, Abrahams sat beaming, flashing a wide smile, no doubt proud for having orchestrated Malcolm's visit to Oxford. Born in Jamaica, Abrahams represented the slow, but growing influx of students of color into Oxford University, and into the Union Society proper. He was not the first president of color of the Union, nor its first from the West Indies. That distinction belonged to a Barbadian named Cameron Tudor, elected in 1942, whom Joseph Goebbels reportedly referred to as a "slave boy in Oxonian robes."[12] It clearly pained Abrahams not to be able to offer Malcolm an honorarium for his talk.

FIGURE 1.2 Oxford Union Society president Eric Abrahams and Malcolm X share a predebate laugh. (*Oxford Mail*)

"We greatly appreciate your gesture," he wrote Malcolm in his letter of invitation, knowing all he could cover was travel and hotel accommodations. On top of this, Malcolm was not to give any interviews while in the United Kingdom, a ban designed to "protect our sponsors." The BBC insisted upon exclusive access to Malcolm over the course of his four-day visit.[13] Reflecting years later upon his invitation to Malcolm, Abrahams described his own sense of militancy at the time:

> [I'd] always followed the American civil rights struggle, and I saw him as very much the person who was making the most sense to me. I didn't believe in those days that nonviolence was going to be the answer. In fact, I really am surprised at the extent to which America, short of a violent overthrow or a violent upsurge, would have agreed to go along with the degree of social changes that have taken place. So my hopes were on Malcolm X, not on Martin Luther King.[14]

Abrahams would be the first to present an argument the night of the debate, affirming the right of people to adopt extreme measures in their defense of liberty. In a sense, Abrahams had been doing so at Oxford, where during the duration of Malcolm's visit, he was not allowed out of his apartment after six in the evening, because of his participation in a campus protest against the arrest of Nelson Mandela (see figure 1.3). Abrahams's form of house arrest, known at Oxford as "gating," was administered by the university proctors, who were particularly displeased with Abrahams for failing to provide his full name to the police, and for his status as an undergraduate. A week before Malcolm's visit, all undergraduates had been banned from organizing any demonstrations against apartheid designed to coincide with the visit of South Africa's ambassador.[15]

FIGURE 1.3 Tariq Ali and Eric Anthony Abrahams, protesting against the South African ambassador's Oxford visit, November 1964. (*Oxford Mail*)

Abrahams's disobedience had the advantageous effect of turning his apartment into an informal debate hall the night of the debate, as Malcolm was said to have held court in the overflowing residence, apparently to the delight of university students.[16] In one of a number of lighthearted moments from the debate, Humphry Berkeley, a Conservative Member of Parliament, who spoke just before Malcolm, chided Abrahams for his speech leading off the debate. "You sir, are not a man given to extremism," Berkeley suggested, decrying the bombast he detected in Abrahams's remarks favoring extremism. "Ask the proctors!" replied Abrahams, to much laughter in the chamber.[17]

Over Abrahams's right shoulder in the official photograph from the debate was a fellow traveler in the radical politics of the day at Oxford. Tariq Ali, like Abrahams, had been gated for his participation in the antiapartheid demonstration the week before Malcolm's visit. By his own admission, Ali had been deeply suspicious of Malcolm upon meeting him. Despite his Pakistani birth, Ali was, and remains, a secularist, and Malcolm's longtime affiliation with the Nation of Islam and its brand of religious fundamentalism led him to question Malcolm's politics. "When we were introduced," Ali recalled in his memoir, "he smiled at my name and said in a soft voice, 'A fellow Muslim?' I shook his hand firmly and whispered in his ear, 'In name only.' He laughed aloud."[18] Indeed, the evening of Malcolm's departure from Oxford provided ample evidence to support Ali's identity as a confirmed apostate. Photographed in the *Oxford Mail* sitting on the floor beside a young co-ed as Abrahams poured champagne into their glasses, Ali reportedly "drank champagne from a slipper" that evening. What's more, "No girls wore topless dresses at the Oxford Union ball, last night," noted the *Mail*, "though the President, Eric Abrahams of St. Peter's College, had said beforehand that at least six could be expected."[19] This was not quite the type of "liberty" up for debate the previous evening.

Ali sat beside Malcolm for the duration of the debate and is one of a handful of people to have written about that night. Years later

Ali would recall, "The entire audience was spellbound by his use of words, his imagery and, surprisingly, his total lack of demagogy."[20] Ali would go on to succeed Abrahams as Union president beginning in the Trinity term at Oxford University. His free-spiritedness perhaps accounted for his reputation on campus as something of an all too well-heeled revolutionary. But there was no mistaking Ali's stance against racial and class injustice and his subsequent career as a radical novelist and filmmaker confirm his youthful sensibilities toward protest and the rise of leftist politics at Oxford. As will be recounted later, Ali was the last person to speak at length with Malcolm after the debate at Oxford. Their conversation was foreboding:

> At 2 am I realized that I was in breach of Proctorial regulations and explained the whys and wherefores to Malcolm. He was truly amazed and laughed aloud. As I was getting ready to leave I shook hands and expressed the hope that we would meet again before too long. He smiled and, without any trace of emotion, said: "I don't think so. By this time next year I'll be dead." I froze, staring at him in disbelief.[21]

In addition to the growing number of students of color from the Commonwealth present at Oxford in 1964 was the tiny contingent of women. In 1964, women made up roughly 16 percent of the student population of Oxford University, compared to 38 percent throughout the rest of the British university system.[22] They were confined in essence to five women's colleges and were not given serious consideration for admission into the men's colleges until the 1960s. Finally, in 1963, women won a majority of votes in the Union to warrant admission.[23] The BBC's coverage of the 1964 debate captured many of the facial expressions from the women in the audience who heard Malcolm X's defense of extremism. Among those in the audience were Suzanne Maiden and Prue Hyman. Maiden, of Somerville College, stands smiling in the official photograph from the debate, directly behind Malcolm. Three persons over to her left is Hyman, also smiling, ever so slightly. In 1964, this was the official portrait of diversity at the Oxford Union Society. It is a window into an ancient world, one pivoting toward the acceptance, however grudgingly, of women, members of the working class, and people of color. Intriguingly, to Malcolm's immediate left is seated his chief combatant during the debate, Humphry Berkeley. While Berkeley was an ostensible conservative at the time, and a Member of Parliament whose political career took a number of ideological turns, his status as a gay man was widely known. Not long after the debate, in 1965, Berkeley sought to legalize homosexual relations throughout the UK.[24] His tête-à-tête with Malcolm at Oxford holds an intriguing underlying story of identity politics, particularly given more recent and controversial interpretations of Malcolm's own sexuality.[25] All the same, despite the staid and almost morosely traditional quality to the official photograph from the debate of December 3, it becomes clear upon reflection just how much the world of Oxford was undergoing transformation. It was Malcolm's great hope that that turn would be driven by the undeniable recognition of the humanity of black people broadly defined and their right to affirm that personhood by any means necessary.

Harlem and Oxford: Racial Change in Miniature

Much of the ineffability of Malcolm X's presence at Oxford was the sense of incongruity inspired by his ties to Harlem. While Malcolm lived in many places—Omaha, Lansing, and Roxbury, to name but a few—he has rightfully become associated with Harlem. As Ossie Davis noted in his now famous eulogy of Malcolm, "Here—at this final hour, in this quiet place—Harlem has come to bid farewell to one of its brightest hopes—extinguished now, and gone from us forever. For Harlem is where he worked and where he struggled and fought—his home of homes, where his heart was, and where his people are—and it is, therefore, most fitting that we meet once again—in Harlem—to share these last moments with him."[26]

Harlem's longstanding tradition of soap-box preaching and public speaking, and the informality of structure attached to street-worn debate, give it a veneer quite different from that of Oxford. There, the rules of debate and orderliness given to speechmaking have become synonymous with "Englishness" in the same way Harlem has long been identified with blackness. And while these efforts at grasping cultural purity belie the truth of messy ethnic and cultural pluralism in both places, there is something to the notion of *georacial* space attached to their history.[27] There has been an almost anthropological sense of Englishness attached to the Oxford Union's adherence to rules, tradition, eccentricity, individuality, and rationality.[28] This seems to run counter to Harlem as home to syncopation, community, modernity, and improvisation. Malcolm was one of the few American figures of the twentieth century to be able to rhetorically navigate the streets of Harlem and the debate hall at Oxford with equal aplomb. Malcolm's ability as a wordsmith and craftsman of language stemmed from the most disparate set of experiences possible. In this way, he represented a Twain-like quality to be not only "*an* American," but "*the* American."

Malcolm received two types of education in public speaking: his time as minister and spokesperson for Elijah Muhammad and his participation in the Norfolk Penal Colony's debate program in Massachusetts. In actuality, Malcolm's first Oxford debate experience probably came during his incarceration, as both Cambridge and Oxford Universities sent debate teams to the Norfolk prison while Malcolm was present.[29] These more formal encounters were layered over with street speeches and debates. At least since the early twentieth century, Harlem had been home to this form of public speaking. The black Socialist leader Hubert Harrison was a pioneer in street-corner oratory in Harlem and set the standard for decades in his ability to attract large crowds and enliven outdoor audiences as early as the First World War.[30] It was on the corner of 135th Street and Lennox Avenue that Harrison and a host of newly arrived West Indian immigrants created the spirited open-speech environment that became synonymous with Harlem. The corner soon became known, appropriately enough, as "the campus."[31]

Undoubtedly, Malcolm would find the Harlem of today radically different than that of 1964. Harlem today is largely devoid of any street peddlers, and increasingly white, and one must strain to glimpse the sense of it as a rhetorical milieu for racial politics and culture. Just a few short years after Malcolm's death, blacks made up nearly two-thirds of Harlem's population. Today, that number is down to just over 40 percent. What's more, Harlem's cachet today has as much to do with its value as one of New York City's few remaining neighborhoods with available and affordable residential spaces, as the city experiences profound shifts in its socioeconomic and ethnic demographics.[32] Oxford has undergone similar changes. In 1964, it was commonplace for students of color to be denied housing in the town on the basis of their color alone. The specter of racial contamination was hardly the preserve of fringe racist organizations, and their arguments were hard to tell apart from those more esteemed in the public eye. "A white guest might be a bit dubious about having a bath after a black man," explained the secretary of the Oxford Association of Hotels and Guest Houses. "Well, I mean there might be diseases...I wouldn't imagine an English mother wanting her daughter to share a room with a black girl student."[33] Today, Oxford's population is disproportionately diverse as compared to the rest of England. Nearly one in five city residents is classified as black or as a member of another minority ethnic population; the city today also has the second highest proportion of people born outside the UK in the South East of England.[34] As will be discussed, Oxford's changes mirror those having taken place in the UK over the past fifty years. In all probability, were Malcolm's visit to Oxford to take place today, it would be far less provocative as a consequence of his racial identity. His religious background would likely be another matter altogether. The *Oxford Mail*'s headline "Black Muslim in Oxford" in 1964 was ominous because of the word "Black." The term "Muslim" then was relatively innocuous, and when Malcolm presented his religious credentials to his Oxford audience, there was a banality to their silence that held a charming innocence.

"The Kind of Problem You Now Face in Britain"

In the spring of 1965 the British government attempted to bring itself up to speed on American race relations, including an assessment of the integration of Puerto Ricans into life in the continental United States. As immigrants of color began to become ever present in British society, the notion was that through careful study and visitations, the UK might learn something of racial integration from its younger cousin. The NAACP's executive director, Roy Wilkins, was eager to assist. His correspondence with a Member of Parliament, Charles Longbottom, in June 1965 is striking in its attempt to offer some solace on what was now becoming more of a "British Dilemma":

> It will be good to see you again and to add a word on our experience over here on the kind of problem you now face in Britain. New York was the first of our states to enact a law against racial discrimination in employment (1945) and this has been followed by a fair housing law. Prior to that time we had for as long as forty years a so-called civil rights law, which, in effect covered treatment of racial minority members in places of public accommodation such as theatres, hotels, restaurants, etc.[35]

The plan was for Maurice Foley, parliamentary undersecretary for economic affairs, to join Longbottom on a visit to "study American racial problems" and arrange for others to visit Puerto Rico to "study Operation Bootstrap," the United States' plan to rapidly industrialize the island. Most of these initial plans fell through over the course of the spring, but it was hoped that "[Foley] may wish to [visit] later in the year in order to study the problems of Puerto Rican immigrants."[36]

In a sense, Malcolm's visits to the UK over the course of three months in late 1964 and early 1965 were for the same purpose. Malcolm was indeed seeking to understand "the kind of problem now facing Britain." His objective was rather different from the NAACP's Wilkins's, however, who was more apt to characterize America's experience with race as troubled but moving forward. Malcolm saw the "nightmare" of the black experience in the United States as a window into the plight of other diasporic blacks—and a source for building racial unity to strengthen the claims of all. From the point of view of US and UK national interests as then defined, prescriptive approaches to resolving racial problems were very much owing to postwar realities for both states. In the UK, imperial identity was undergoing serious transformation, as newly independent states and their peoples began to assert their political interests at home and within the UK itself. At the same time, the United States saw its "dilemma" as part of the peculiar residual legacy of slavery and an equally daunting feature of Cold War politics. Liberalism's compelling argument against communism had been its emphasis on individual liberty and the universal applicability of the social compact. In the face of Soviet power and the appeal of socialist policies, American racism struck a most discordant note to many newly liberated peoples throughout the world. As the legal historian Mary L. Dudziak points out in her book *Cold War Civil Rights*, "domestic civil rights cases would quickly become international crises" as the figurative votes of more than half the globe were up for grabs.[37]

From the vantage point of British authorities, Malcolm X's visit to Oxford was clearly an unwelcome reminder of the role race was playing in British national and local politics. England had been changing, becoming "browner" since the 1940s and 1950s. The racial and religious dimension of change was seen as unsustainable in some quarters, as the "projected" racial makeup of Great Britain was forecast by the Cabinet Commonwealth Migrants Committee in 1961.[38] Such fears had come to be exploited, if not realized, in evaluating more recent figures of ethnic populations. Margaret Thatcher's well-remembered line from a 1978 interview, in which she described the prospect of being "swamped" with immigrants, demonstrated how racial politics had evolved in the UK since 1964.[39] The demographic changes had social implications to be sure, as shoe manufacturers in 1966 were "asked to refrain from using the word 'nigger' to describe dark brown footwear [as in *nigger brown*] so as not to offend coloured people."[40] When Malcolm playfully joked during his Oxford address about the assumption that he might have dined alone with a white female student, the laughter was decidedly nervous. Interracial couples were hardly unheard of at Oxford, but like nearly all things related to race in the early 1960s, their reality was distinctly new and, to a great many, off-putting. As the British political scientist Paul Rich has written:

> The loss of empire came as a profound psychological shock to a society that had grown used to having colonial possessions, despite its ignorance of their nature and extent. The sense of imperial mission and "trusteeship" and governance over "backward races" extended, however, only to the colonial sphere and became difficult to reapply back within the imperial metropolis itself once a series of black communities, with links back to former colonial possessions, had begun to emerge in its midst.[41]

By the end of the Second World War, the UK was in a far different place than it had been when John Stuart Mill published ruminations on British superiority in the pamphlet *England and Ireland* in 1868. Mills's conjectures included the argument that nations such as India and Jamaica were "unfit for liberty."[42] This was but one supposition that Malcolm sought to address at Oxford. As Malcolm warned, extremism, like liberty, had to be understood outside of the context of its association with race or ethnicity; it had to be valued for its inherent and universal worth. Despite efforts to meld party and national image into the ephemera of racial nothingness—as depicted in the famous Conservative Party campaign poster "Labour Says He's Black. Tories Say He's British"—the politics of race as practiced in the early decades after the war were anything but postracial.[43] The unasked question in the poster is, of course, what does *he* say? Malcolm sought to give voice to that stick-figure image of blackness.

As will be detailed in the next chapter, by 1964, racial politics emerged in Britain as a focal point of a national election. It was, notably, the first time the issue had been introduced by the dean of British electoral politics research, David Butler, in his review of national elections.[44] As noted in Butler's study of 1964, immigration and its connection to race had unexpectedly moved to the heart of national elections:

> The Commonwealth Immigrants Act, which came into force in July 1962, made explicit the fact that colour had become an issue in British politics. Although the Act controlled immigration from all Commonwealth countries, it was in effect aimed at the coloured Commonwealth, as the exemption of the Irish seemed to underline. The bill was vigorously opposed in the House of Commons by the Labour Party on the grounds that it was an anti-colour measure and that it threatened the whole Commonwealth idea. The conservatives argued that the bill, by anticipating the rise of racial tension, would avoid it.[45]

The issue was particularly acute in the industrial town of Smethwick, where the slogan "If you want a nigger neighbor vote Labour" was employed in March 1964.[46] The Conservative candidate there, Peter Griffiths, had favored a five-year moratorium on immigration. While it was debated at the time whether or not the winds of racial backlash were at his back, Griffiths went on to defeat Labour's Gordon Walker in October. Walker was no ordinary Labour candidate. He was Harold Wilson's first choice for foreign secretary in the incoming Labour government, making his defeat all the more striking. Griffiths, meanwhile, denied using the offensive slogan in question but likewise refused to repudiate it on the grounds that it was a "manifestation of popular feeling."[47] Labour was indeed in a difficult position on the question, as only 10 percent of those polled by Gallup supported unrestricted immigration (to a combined 88 percent favoring some form of unilaterally or negotiated control or ban).[48] As Smethwick was made up of a growing number of Indians and West Indians, it drew Malcolm's interest, and he would visit the city in February 1965, with a BBC crew in tow. He was assassinated just ten days later.

As so much has been written about Malcolm's hajj and journeys to both Africa and the Islamic world in 1964, there has been a tendency to underplay his objectives in Europe toward the end of his life. And while Malcolm was eerily prescient about his own death, he was nonetheless working toward political goals that were as important to him in Paris and London as they were to him back in New York and Washington. If we are to understand Oxford as crucial for assessing not only Malcolm's ultimate political philosophy and worldview, but also the nature of an emerging and dynamic transformation of racial politics in the United States and United Kingdom, it is important to look at the week in Malcolm's life leading up to the debate. The week that began in Paris and ended outside his hotel, talking with a young Tariq Ali into the wee hours of the morning, in Oxford.

Paris

Malcolm's trip to France was part of his larger developing strategy of converting the American civil rights issue into an international discussion of human rights. By speaking to the black diaspora in Paris, he was hoping to galvanize the kind of support he hoped to elicit in England and other parts of Europe. Paris and Oxford were part of the same line of reasoning. The black struggle in America would never gain the kind of traction necessary for resolving the historic problems of African Americans if it were restricted to the public opinion and legal jurisdiction of the United States.

Malcolm's speech at the Salle de la Mutualité was scheduled for Sunday, November 23. The day's headlines in *Le Monde* had to have interested him, had he read them. "Une Année Sans Kennedy" ("A Year Without Kennedy") ran the foreign bulletin on the left column. It was indeed the day after the first anniversary of Kennedy's assassination in Dallas. Malcolm's life changed forever with his "Chickens coming home to roost" remarks about the slain American president. He had been ostensibly "silenced" by Elijah Muhammad for those remarks, and more importantly, they marked the effective end to his tenure as national minister within the Nation of Islam. After an article on Sino-Russian relations, an article appeared on the Congo: "Le Sort des Otages de Stanleyville" ("The Fate of the Stanleyville Hostages"). The Congo crisis, as it quickly came to be called, greatly interested Malcolm, and it was a continual point of reference in his speeches leading up to and including Oxford. When white hostages became a chief concern of the European press, Malcolm argued that "they give me the impression that they attach more importance to a white hostage and a white death than they do the death of a human being despite the color of his skin."[49] By the time Malcolm spoke in the Oxford debate hall, some sixty white hostages had been killed. His remarks on this proved to be both controversial and, upon explanation, surprisingly well received.

By the day of his speech at Mutualité, Malcolm had already been in Paris five days and would remain nearly a full week. He was well into his fourth month away from the United States, with most of this time spent in Africa. As stated, Paris represented more than just a leisurely stopover for Malcolm. It was his opportunity to connect with the black American and African diaspora in France—and to redirect attention to the global dimension of "human" rather than civil rights. There had been a long and rich tradition of black literary and political figures traveling to, and indeed, living in, Paris. Pablo Picasso had in fact designed the cover of the program to the First International Congress of Black Writers and Artists in Paris in 1956 and remained close to a number of black artistic figures well into the 1960s.[50] In 1963, James Baldwin and others were organizing around the upcoming March on Washington, which led to what one historian has called "the only time that blacks in Paris actually staged a public march for civil rights"—a silent march across the Seine to the US embassy in support of the historic demonstration back home. Malcolm's newly formed Organization of Afro-American Unity also managed to form a chapter in Paris, as the global dimension of the black civil rights movement began to percolate.[51]

Malcolm was introduced to this small but vibrant expatriate community, meeting with Richard Wright's widow, Ellen, and their youngest daughter, Julia.[52] He also met with the student leader Carlos Moore, an Afro-Cuban with whom Malcolm conferred over how to assist the Congolese rebels in Stanleyville.[53] Moore also served as an ad hoc translator for Malcolm, who was just learning to speak French, a handicap in his efforts to reach out to the black diaspora that troubled him quite a bit.[54] The African American writer Chester Himes, then living in Paris, and very much attuned to Malcolm's politics, recounted Malcolm's impact on black Paris at the time:

> There were a lot of young American blacks in Paris at that time who were devoutly interested in Malcolm X, who had returned from Mecca. Some claimed to be his followers and more or less worshiped him, others wanted to know him to become his followers; the black women oldtimers on the Paris scene were all trying to seduce him. There were scores of black men who claimed to be watching Malcolm for the CIA.[55]

Himes noted that Malcolm greeted the crowd of hundreds outside Mutualité after the talk and shook hands with all those who sought him out.[56] Julia Wright and Carlos Moore, among others, organized

Malcolm's return to Paris in February.[57] Their efforts were thwarted at the last minute as the French government refused Malcolm entry on February 9, 1965.

France, like England, had had its own growing difficulties related to race and "ethnic immigration" since the Second World War. The Negritude movement, a cultural response to the denial of black equality and intellectual creativity, had been in full swing since the war and became identified with Alioune Diop, who founded and became the editor of Presence Africaine in Paris in 1947.[58] It was Diop who organized the first Congress of Negro Writers and Artists in Paris in 1956. Malcolm later reached out to Diop in an effort to win the support of African nations for the American civil rights struggle. This diasporic approach was at the heart of why Malcolm was in Paris—and later Oxford and London within the span of a week at the end of 1964. Unlike in London, however, the contours of a "Paris Noir" could barely be defined. In the mid-1960s, black Paris was more of a literary ideal—an almost aesthetic realm of artists, activists, and passers-by—than a definable geographical community. Over time, as the demand for labor skyrocketed in France after the war years, immigration became a fundamental dimension of the French economy. In 1946, there were 82,818 immigrants to France. By 1956, the year of the First Congress of Black Writers in Paris, there were 136,004. Before long, nearly one in five was arriving from North Africa.[59] Today, the Parisian neighborhood most defined by the large presence of Africans—sometimes known as "Goutte d'Or" and others as "Chateau Rouge" or "Barbès"—is a much more significant and vibrant enclave than Malcolm would have experienced during his visit in 1964. This "Little Africa," in Paris' Eighteenth Arrondissement, popularized by the American-born Jake Lamar in his novel *Rendezvous Eighteenth*, reflects the powerful growth in immigration in France over the last fifty years. Its diversity today in some respects belies Malcolm's black Nationalist or pan-Africanist vision, as Senegalese, Cameroons, Cote Ivoirians, and others live and work among one another, but not always in easy unison or with identical political interests.[60] Interestingly enough, those advocating for minority rights in France today have, like their UK counterparts nearly fifty years ago, undertaken to visit and study the United States' handling of ethnic diversity. One early recommendation, it seems, is to end the French policy of failing to keep statistics on different racial or ethnic groups. The idea of assimilation, so coveted, but ever elusive, remains highly contentious, not only in France, but in nearly all of Europe.[61]

While Malcolm had a clear purpose in supporting a nascent African community in France, and undoubtedly sought to connect with the historic and elite corps of African American expatriates in Paris, it is also undeniable that his speech at Mutualité lacked the clarity, cohesiveness, and depth that would be on display only ten days later in Oxford. By Malcolm's own admission, words had begun to fail him toward the end of his second lengthy trip abroad in 1964. Whether it was Lyndon Johnson's election as president that served to blunt Malcolm's critiques of American racial injustice, given his overwhelming support among African Americans, or simple fatigue, the Paris speech was not Malcolm at his best.[62] He did make some significant and, for Malcolm, paradigm-shattering observations in the question-and-answer period, and those sentiments do suggest an intellectual pathway beyond Black Nationalism, one that Oxford would ultimately underscore.

Malcolm at the Salle de la Mutualité

Jacques Amalric of *Le Monde* provided a bit of theatrical flair in his account of Malcolm's speech, noting how his *pied-de-poule* styled suit and *barbe soignée* ("tidy beard") gave him the appearance of a modern jazz quartet intellectual. All the same, *Le Monde* did give a short but accurate account of some of Malcolm's major points that evening.[63] No major American media outlets reported on the speech. Ruth Porter, of *The Militant*, was the only American member of the press to write any account of Malcolm's lecture. Noting that Malcolm's visit followed on the heels only weeks before of Langston Hughes, Porter painted a picture of what the hall at Mutualité that evening was like:

> There wasn't a square inch of unoccupied space in the meeting room. The seats were filled an hour before the lecture was scheduled to begin. The "late" arrivals stood or sat on the floor. When not another human being could be jammed into the hall, the crowd spilled into the corridors, hoping to stand within earshot. Those who arrived on time could not find standing room in the corridors and had to leave. The speaker himself could barely push into the room over the assorted legs of those on the floor. Africans, Americans black and white, European leftists of all persuasions, representatives of the press, all were intensely interested in what Malcolm X would say.[64]

Because the recording of the speech was so poor and remaining excerpts are disjointed in different accounts, we have no lasting, single, continuous representation from Malcolm's lecture in Paris. Porter's account does highlight Malcolm's effort to split his political and religious affiliations—the "two hats" he writes of in his diary. "Tonight, I am speaking for the [organization] that is non-religious," he said at the outset of his address.[65] Malcolm was not rejecting the value of religion in the lives of blacks, or others, for that matter. Instead, he was seeking to build the widest bridge to those interested in the liberation of Africa, and racial justice in the United States. When asked during the question-and-answer portion of the evening whether or not he was a Muslim before joining the "Black Muslims," Malcolm responded, "A man's choice of religion is his personal business."[66]

Later, when queried in French about his support for interracial love ("Est-il vrai que vous êtes opposé aux marriages interraciaux?"), Malcolm compared it to a matter of faith.[67] "How can anyone be against love? Whoever a person wants to love that's their business—that's like their religion."[68] These were clear departures from Malcolm's former racial cosmology, one that banned inter-racial romance. Moreover, these views presaged a more inclusive Malcolm, one who at Oxford proffered a sweeping possibility for racial solidarity and collective militancy. What Malcolm's ideology could not bear was the false pretense of brotherhood. It is why in Paris, just one year after the assassination of Kennedy, he could not pass on the opportunity to disavow the weaknesses and hypocrisy of liberalism as he saw it:

> [Colonialism] is like a person when he's playing football: when he's trapped he doesn't give the ball up—he passes it to someone who is in the clear.... The United States was in the clear, so all the colonial powers did was pass the ball to the United States, and it was caught by John F. Kennedy.... And if an African thinks that an American is going to come on the African continent with some Peace Corps and Crossroads and these other outfits and help you, you tell me why she won't help us and we have slaved for her and have died for her.[69]

In short order, Malcolm made a similar attack on President Johnson, arguing that the American system was in actuality a global system, one that benefits from the appearance of liberal altruism. "I have to say this," Malcolm argued. "Those who claim to be enemies of the system were on their hands and knees waiting for Johnson to get elected because he's supposed to be a man of peace; and he has troops invading the Congo right now and invading Saigon and places where other countries have pulled their troops out."[70]

In her reporting from that evening, Porter captured something that did not make its way into *Presence Africaine*'s or other later accounts of Malcolm's speech. It was a similarly based attack against liberalism, one that drew ringing applause according to Porter. "Efforts of 'liberals' to solve our problems for us," said Malcolm, "have been efforts to make us become more American than African. They have no desire or intention to solve the race problem because it would mean giving up power—and no one ever gives up power. It has to be taken from them."[71] Foreshadowing his Oxford debate, Malcolm addressed a question concerning his movement's extremism. "Number one," he began, "if we are extremists we're not ashamed of it. In fact, the conditions that our people suffer are extreme and an extreme illness cannot be cured with a moderate medicine."[72]

Despite Malcolm's uneven presentation, Chester Himes and others present were struck by the success of the evening and Malcolm's performance. Another meeting in Paris was quickly arranged not long after Malcolm left.[73] Alas, "I took [my wife] home," recalled Chester Himes, "and I never saw Malcolm again."[74]

The Lost Jewel

For many years, Malcolm's contributions to the language, rhetoric, and movement toward civil rights in America were underestimated or ignored altogether. That has largely changed in recent years. Nevertheless, historians still have difficulty in placing him within the broader context of the civil rights movement. In his prolific work on Malcolm's life, Manning Marable properly emphasizes two critical speeches given by Malcolm; these are his "Message to the Grassroots" and "The Ballot or the Bullet."[75] Without a doubt, both of these speeches capture quintessential elements of Malcolm's political philosophy and his true genius for employing colorful, yet direct language. The "Ballot or the Bullet" speech, delivered in Cleveland on April 3, 1964, demonstrates Malcolm's powerful oratorical gifts. The juxtaposition of ballots and bullets (much like the use of "house" and "field" Negroes in the "Grassroots" speech) provided the kind of unsettling ambiguity Malcolm loved employing. His signature catchphrase—"By any means necessary"—suggests the same thing. It was in the Cleveland speech that Malcolm gave his retort to the notion of an American identity for blacks in the United States:

> Well, I am one who doesn't believe in deluding myself. I'm not going to sit at your table and watch you eat, with nothing on my plate, and call myself a diner. Sitting at the table doesn't make you a diner, unless you eat some of what's on that plate. Being here in America doesn't make you an American. Being born here in America doesn't make you an American. Why, if birth made you an American, you wouldn't need any legislation, you wouldn't need any amendments to the Constitution, you wouldn't be faced with any civil-rights filibustering in Washington, D.C., right now.... I'm speaking as a victim of this American system. And I see America through the eyes of a victim. I don't see any American dream; I see an American nightmare.[76]

Malcolm's last great speech as a member of the Nation of Islam, and among the most important touchstone's of his legacy, is his "Message to the Grass Roots," delivered just a few weeks before Kennedy was murdered in Dallas and Malcolm's subsequent suspension from his post as national spokesman for the Honorable Elijah Muhammad. It is a fiery, revolutionary speech—and contains some of the best-known turns of phrase used by Malcolm. Here we have a host of dualities employed to shame fearful blacks: the image of the house Negro and the field Negro; the distinction between the Negro revolution and other revolutions; the image of black coffee being diluted with white cream. All are on display in this Detroit address, including his condemnation of what he called the "Farce on Washington." "When James Baldwin came in from Paris, they wouldn't let him talk," said Malcolm. "Burt Lancaster read the speech that Baldwin was supposed to make; they wouldn't let Baldwin get up there, because they know Baldwin is liable to say anything."[77]

A case may be made that both of these speeches, and others, including "The Black Revolution" and his last major address after his home was firebombed in February 1965, are his best or most appealing, for any number of reasons. But they all, to one degree or another, lack what the Oxford address provided. Malcolm at Oxford represented the most comprehensive, best articulated, and clearest sense of his personal and political vision on the future of race relations—not only as a domestic concern, but also a global one. Oxford and its audience were interactive, at times combative, and challenging in terms of a venue that demanded not only passion and skill, but grace, precision, and substantive argument. The Oxford address certainly contained a number of elements from Malcolm's old racial narratives, but it largely was rooted in the future, one in which Malcolm was increasingly open to a revolutionary politics absent of overarching racial dogmatism. It was a future in which race would matter, but not be *the* matter altogether. Finally, as we will see, Oxford suggests a pivotal moment in human history, as the majority of the world's population begins to unyoke itself from colonial or imperial rule while simultaneously struggling with, or anticipating, the challenges of racially pluralistic societies developing along egalitarian lines. The demands of the future, rather than a mere articulation of present or past problems, brought the very best out of Malcolm X—and it happened in Oxford. In this most basic sense, the speech represents what can only be called the lost jewel of the American civil rights movement. It is precisely because in that moment—one Dr. King would step into in 1967 and 1968—the nature of America's racial challenges could no longer stand on their own. They had to be wed to the greater struggle for human dignity on a global scale.

By the time Malcolm was introduced, the audience had heard from Eric Abrahams; Christie Davies of the Cambridge Union, who was substituting for Edward Heath, MP, who was late arriving from Parliament and would offer commentary that evening from the studios of the BBC; the Scottish nationalist and communist Hugh MacDiarmid; and finally, Humphry Berkeley. While MacDiarmid's ode to extremism included William Blake's line "the road of excess leads to the palace of wisdom," there was little that Malcolm could have found appealing in Humphry Berkeley's speech. In response to Malcolm's support for the motion in question, it seemed Berkeley took personal offense at, or at least liberties with, Malcolm's personal identity. By Tariq Ali's account of the debate, Berkeley engaged in a bit of ridicule, asking Malcolm why he chose or preferred "X" to "C" or even "Z."[78] There is no full broadcast video of the BBC's coverage from the debate, but Malcolm does address the questioning of his name's origin. And he can be seen on the edited tape offering a hint of a smile at Berkeley's description of himself as "North America's leading exponent of apartheid." At this point Ali, seated beside Malcolm, turns toward him, seemingly to assess the impact of Berkeley's blow. Malcolm appears calm, head resting pensively on his hand, smiling. Ali turns away, satisfied that all appears well. Moments later, Malcolm can be seen taking notes, almost feverishly, engrossed in his preparations. He is up next.[79]

What then transpires is a near thirty-minute exposition that is perhaps the best encapsulation of Malcolm X's ultimate views on race, American politics, and what can only be called universal human rights. While clearly Malcolm's politics were evolving and we cannot know for certain whether, let alone where, his ideology might have taken root, it is hard to identify a speech better than Oxford to identify comprehensively where Malcolm stood on so many philosophical questions. And by virtue of his posture at Oxford, his humor and evident pleasure in delivering the speech—even down to receiving Berkeley's barbs—he appears almost preternaturally content. In this respect, Oxford offers a unique window into Malcolm's personal and overwhelmingly private disposition. In this moment, one that briefly punctured his own self-aware confrontation with death, Malcolm X appears happy. With his notes in his coat pocket, he rises from his seat as the Union president Abrahams announces, "It is with great pleasure that I call upon Mr. Malcolm X to speak fifth, in favor of the motion."

Chapter 2

Extremism: "The revolution is now on the inside of the house"

As Malcolm took his position at the speaker's rostrum amid a sea of faces looking up at him, his calm demeanor and deliberate beginning masked a fury burning within (figure 2.1). Some time after the debate he confided that Humphry Berkeley's remarks had so enflamed him that "it took an effort of will to keep myself from trembling."[1] "Mr. Chairman," Malcolm slowly began, "tonight is the first night that I've ever had an opportunity to be as near to conservatives as I am."[2] With this opening salvo, Malcolm helped himself immensely. The line elicited the expected laughter from the audience and at once undermined the notion that Malcolm X—"America's leading exponent of Apartheid," as Berkeley had labeled him—was nothing more than a shrill, humorless man, hell-bent on violence. It also allowed Malcolm a moment to gather himself before commencing with his formal remarks. Still, even before he could get to his perfunctory statement thanking the Union for inviting him, Malcolm couldn't help initiating his own attack. Composing himself, he wasted no time getting at Berkeley:

> And the speaker who preceded me—First, I want to thank you for the invitation to come here to the Oxford Union. The speaker who preceded me is one of the best excuses that I know to prove our point concerning the necessity, sometimes, of extremism in the defense of liberty, why it is no vice, and why moderation in the pursuit of justice is no virtue. I don't say that about him personally, but that *type* is the—[*Laughter and applause*].[3]

FIGURE 2.1 View of debate chamber, Oxford Union, night of debate on extremism. (*Oxford Mail*)

In fairness to Berkeley, his address contained considerably more than a number of barbs directed toward Malcolm. Yet his two chief lines of attack—one ridiculing Malcolm's name and the other comparing him to an apartheid leader of South Africa—unsurprisingly drew Malcolm's fire. "He's right. *X* is not my real name," Malcolm responded. "But if you study history, you'll find why no Black man in the Western Hemisphere knows his real name. Some of *his* ancestors kidnapped *our* ancestors from Africa and took us into the Western Hemisphere and sold us there, and our names were stripped from us and so today we don't know who we really are. I'm one of those who admit it, and so I just put *X* up there to keep from wearing his name."[4]

With this strong personal rebuttal delivered, Malcolm then moved to correct the notion that he remained a racial separatist, suggesting that Berkeley had been "misinformed." "I don't believe in any form of apartheid. I don't believe in any form of segregation.

I don't believe in any form of racialism," he protested, before drawing a line: "But at the same time, I don't endorse a person as being right just because his skin is white. And oftimes, when you find people like this—I mean that type—[*Laughter*]."⁵ In these few lines, Malcolm had clearly struck a nerve with the audience, who were soon anticipating his "that type" line. It was Shakespearian in its conferral of "honor" upon Berkeley, who assumed the role of Brutus, as Malcolm skillfully played the aggrieved Antony. Malcolm's repetitive qualifier drew upon a long history of African American rhetoric and was but one feature of his speech that demonstrated his gifts as a public speaker. In his classic essay "On Repetition in Black Culture," James A. Snead described the type of rejoinder provided by Malcolm as a form of "cut" that takes the audience and speech into a more meaningful place:

> Both preacher and congregation employ the "cut." The preacher "cuts" his own speaking in interrupting himself with a phrase such as "praise God" [or with Malcolm here, "*that type*"]....The listeners, in responding to the preacher's calls at random intervals, produce each time they "cut" a slight shift in the texture of the performance.⁶

It is the cutting off of "people like this" with "I mean that type" that invites the audience to participate in the verbal lashing being administered. Malcolm employs this cutting technique some four times at Oxford, ultimately compelling a member of the audience, not unlike a referee in a boxing match, to implore a halt to the attack upon Berkeley. Tony Abrahams, who perhaps had the best view of the hall that night as president of the Oxford Union Society, recalled those exchanges years later. "I have never been as sorry for a man as I was for Humphry Berkeley that night," he said, "because Malcolm took his speech and, I mean, he just tore him up."⁷

Sadly, very few people outside the debate hall, if any, ever saw Malcolm X's opening remarks at Oxford. The BBC carefully edited out much of the speech, bringing viewers into Malcolm's talk at its halfway point. One of his best lines of the night—a retort to a member of the audience—was rendered nonsensical by the broadcast's lead-in to the speech. To further complicate matters, Malcolm was introduced to the BBC's world audience that evening as "one of the most mysterious and unusual figures probably ever to come to Oxford Union." This statement was quickly succeeded by a selective review of Malcolm's biography, with only the most cursory acknowledgment of his religious and philosophical changes since his separation from the Nation of Islam.[8] By the time Malcolm approached the podium, he was once again inevitably engaged in rhetorical combat, not only with his ideological opponents, but also with those who controlled the manner in which his politics were framed.

The political and rhetorical paths taken by Malcolm in the last year of his life were truly astounding. His acceptance of interracial marriage in Paris, his rejection of racial separatism at Oxford, and, indeed, his acerbic, but not demagogic, wit all reflected a growing maturity and dynamism as a speaker. More important, his command of both language and the issues at Oxford demonstrated an ability to remain uncompromisingly militant in his calls for racial justice while extending the sphere of his political reach. It is not surprising, then, that Berkeley had such a difficult time pigeonholing Malcolm as a wild-eyed extremist at Oxford. Some of this was because, as Malcolm suggested, his performance ran counter to his media-distorted image. And, equally important, a good deal of it was because Malcolm had simply changed.

Dallas to San Francisco

It is now well established that Malcolm's break with the Nation of Islam (NOI) had been under way long before his official departure from the organization in March of 1964. By early 1963, political differences as well as personal disagreements among the Nation's hierarchy, including Elijah Muhammad, had been a considerable source of division.[9] Nevertheless, Malcolm continued to make provocative and, at times, irresponsible statements to the press and in his public addresses. These were partly political calculations designed to appease the NOI's leadership, ever watchful of Malcolm for signs of heretical departures from the Nation's core doctrine. At other times, Malcolm's statements were offered to prick at white sensibilities—to, in effect, deny any apologia for black anger in the face of racial injustice in the United States. These missives helped earn Malcolm the reputation as an extremist, an identity not created out of whole cloth by the media. When in the aftermath of the brutal police killing of an unarmed NOI member in Los Angeles in April of 1962 Malcolm attributed divine justice to the crash of an Air France flight carrying 120 white passengers, his frustrations with the NOI's failure to respond militantly led him down a dark rhetorical path.[10] Calling the crash "a very beautiful thing" in June of 1962, he was asked about it nearly a year later, in an interview with Alex Haley in *Playboy*:

> PLAYBOY: How do you reconcile your disavowal of hatred with the announcement you made last year that Allah had brought you "the good news" that 120 white Atlantans had just been killed in an air crash en route to America from Paris?
>
> MALCOLM X: Sir, as I see the law of justice, it says as you sow, so shall you reap. The white man has reveled as the rope snapped the black men's necks. He has reveled around the lynching fire. It's only right for the black man's true God, Allah, to defend us—and for us to be joyous because our God manifests his ability to inflict pain on our enemy.[11]

By the time of the Oxford debate, Malcolm was defending militancy to be sure but not "any indiscriminate killing." He was seeking to eradicate an image he himself had contributed to—one that the media had little appetite in revisiting. In speaking at Oxford of the killing of some sixty white hostages in Stanleyville in the Congo, Malcolm argued, "I don't encourage any acts of murder, nor do I glorify in anybody's death....Nor does the death of so many people go by me without creating some kind of emotion."[12] Malcolm was now qualifying extremism, making it a question of the legitimate versus wanton use of force. This was a difficult needle to thread for Malcolm, particularly given his widely reported remarks about John F. Kennedy's murder. Despite Elijah Muhammad's nationwide decree to his ministers to refuse comment to the press about Kennedy's assassination in November of 1963, Malcolm attempted to dance around the topic at a New York rally, before crossing the line and seeming to rejoice in the president's death. The *New York Times* reported on the remarks, which had a deleterious effect not only upon Malcolm's already troubled relations within the NOI, but also upon his nearly calcified image as an extremist:

> Malcolm X, a leader of the Black Muslims, yesterday characterized the assassination of President Kennedy as an instance of "the chickens coming home to roost." Accusing Mr. Kennedy of "twiddling his thumbs" at the killing of South Vietnamese President Ngo Dinh Diem and his brother, Ngo Dinh Nu, Malcolm X told a Black Muslim rally at the Manhattan Center that he "never foresaw that the chickens would come home to roost so soon." He added: "Being an old farm boy myself, chickens coming home to roost never did make me sad; they've always made me glad."[13]

The *Times* reported the story on December 2, nearly one year to the day before the Oxford speech. Malcolm would spend the next year—indeed the rest of his life—clarifying his position as an advocate of "the right kind of extremism," as he described it at Oxford, as opposed to "the other kind," which ran counter to his principles of justice. That he fared so well a year later at the Oxford debate is testament to his gifts as an orator to be sure, but also as an individual committed to radical change and personal introspection. As the

New Year approached, it was clear that the issue of extremism was going to be central to the way American politics was analyzed and, to a degree, conducted. The debate over political radicalism would indeed be equally salient in the United Kingdom in the British national elections. As Malcolm X's efforts to recast himself were launched, an intriguing set of strands of American and British political thought were woven together at Oxford by year's end.

Goldwater

The journalist Theodore White captured Barry Goldwater's politics well in his classic work on the 1964 presidential election. "Goldwater thought of himself," wrote White in 1965, "and still does, not as a man prepared to or even desiring to run and administer the government of the United States, but as leader of a cause."[14] That cause was American conservatism as best defined by its opposition to New Deal politics and policies. Goldwater's more libertarian bent did not emerge until his second stint in the United States Senate, when the religious Right in the United States began to assert itself during the 1980s. This later incarnation of Goldwater had indeed become so identified with moderation by the New Right's standards that the Arizona senator was a thorn in the side of none other than President Ronald Reagan. "[Goldwater's] raising h—l as chairman of Intelligence [committee]," wrote Reagan in his diary, "because of the harbor mining in Nicaragua—says he was never briefed." Reagan goes on to note how Goldwater's actions will "bring joy to the Soviets & Cubans."[15] The hard right turn in American conservatism had inexplicably passed Goldwater by. Yet during the presidential campaign of 1964, Goldwater was the personification of American conservatism and, in many respects, the most recognizable voice for the nation's extremism. It is perhaps the chief reason why Malcolm thought a Goldwater victory desirable; it would force the inevitable confrontation between the forces of racial progress and oppression. In his

"Message to the Grass Roots," Malcolm described the role moderate leaders played in repressing black anger. His target here was black leadership, but Malcolm often invoked the analogy to reject white liberal leadership's presumably progressive role in racial matters. It is why Lyndon Johnson's election cast such a pall over him:

> It's like when you go to the dentist, and the man's going to take your tooth. You're going to fight him when he starts pulling. So he squirts some stuff in your jaw called novocaine, to make you think they're not doing anything to you. So you sit there and because you've got all that novocaine in your jaw, you suffer—peacefully. Blood running all down your jaw, and you don't know what's happening. Because someone has taught you to suffer—peacefully.[16]

In a sense, Goldwater and Malcolm were both victims of their fetish for the *mot juste*. Goldwater's acceptance speech at the Republican National Convention in July of 1964 was laden with wonderfully evocative turns of phrase, such as the liberal state leading the United States toward a "swampland of collectivism," while satisfying the American public with "bread and circuses." These evocative lines delivered at San Francisco's Cow Palace were ultimately eclipsed by Goldwater's statement near the end of his speech, one delivered to great howls and applause: "I would remind you that extremism in the defense of liberty is no vice," Goldwater said to building applause. "And let me remind you also, that moderation in the pursuit of justice is no virtue."[17] Goldwater's "extremism" line was widely seen as an open embrace of the militant Right in America, including organizations such as the John Birch Society and Ku Klux Klan. Moderate Republicans at the convention, still a formidable faction in 1964, attempted to denounce the Party's connection to extremism but were ultimately shouted down.[18] Fifteen years later in his memoirs, Goldwater blamed governors Nelson Rockefeller and William Scranton, along with moderates George Romney and Henry Cabot Lodge, for his overwhelming defeat in November. As he recounted in his fittingly named *With No Apologies*, Goldwater was called up to Eisenhower's hotel the morning after his acceptance speech to explain himself. The former president was understandably concerned about Goldwater's remarks.[19] In defending extremism—the line from the speech owes its origins to Cicero, it was later argued—Goldwater had unabashedly linked himself with the far right wing of his party. It was, in 1964, a losing proposition.[20]

For his part, Malcolm expressed admiration for, if not agreement with, Goldwater's position. "Goldwater, as a man, I respected for speaking out his true convictions—something rarely done in politics today. He wasn't whispering to racists and smiling at integrationists."[21] Unfortunately for Goldwater, Republicans were slow to build up their party infrastructure in the South and were still paying somewhat for President Eisenhower's intervention in Little Rock in 1957. It was the one region that showed support for Goldwater. Despite the astounding 90 percent loss in the Electoral College, and 60 percent defeat in the popular vote, Republicans were not without hope for the future.[22] In some respects it was fitting that Malcolm would indirectly address Goldwater's party politics at Oxford. "I have more respect for a man who lets me know where he stands, even if he's wrong, than the one who comes up like an angel and is nothing but a devil," said Malcolm to great applause.[23] As will be discussed, Malcolm revisited a well-worn line of attack at Oxford, one directed toward Democrats and liberals, who, he argued, pay only lip service to the cause of liberty for African Americans. In his Machiavellian construction of politics, Malcolm always took the side of the lion over the fox.

Goldwater's line about extremism was quickly picked up abroad and was, of course, adopted by the Oxford Union as a timely topic for debate. The Oxford University student newspaper, *Isis*, had in fact opted to present a more complete image of Goldwater days before the American elections, so as not to leave British students with a one-dimensional view of the United States senator. Malcolm would enjoy no such deference. "[A]part from the truly lunatic fringe in American society," the *Isis* noted, "the typical Goldwater fanatic is no fascist."[24] These were meant to be encouraging words. By late October of 1964, Goldwater found himself buried under an avalanche of reporting in America that reinforced his endorsement of political extremism. For the Johnson campaign, it proved a boon to a Democratic Party, which was increasingly divided on the issue of race. The *New York Times'* Andrew Hacker's lengthy piece on the political mainstream in America was representative of Goldwater's challenges. "This year's [Republican] experiment," wrote Hacker two months before the election, "is betting that there are many Americans—among them many who have hitherto voted Democratic—who are willing to give their votes to a man who promises to keep Negroes in their place."[25] Roy Wilkins, executive director of the NAACP, went further, predicting that a Goldwater victory would lead to a "police state" in America.[26] Undoubtedly, Malcolm did not view Johnson as a champion of black civil rights— a status LBJ now holds among most presidential historians. Yet there is a good deal of complexity to his view here, as Malcolm was a strong proponent of the Civil Rights Act, signed by Johnson in July of 1964. What is most germane, however, is that Malcolm saw Goldwater's opposition to the act as a truer reflection of what white Americans would ultimately countenance and thus as a more effective tool for rallying support for a more radical racial politics. Unlike Wilkins, Malcolm saw America as already exhibiting a kind of police state—one that no individual or group should passively accept. Malcolm's defense of extremism at Oxford began with this universal perspective:

> I think the only way one can really determine whether or not extremism in defense of liberty is justified, is not to approach it as an American or a European or an African or an Asian, but as a human being. If we look upon it as different types, immediately we begin to think in terms of extremism being good for one and bad for another, or bad for one and good for another. But if we look

upon it, if we look upon ourselves as human beings, I doubt that anyone will deny that extremism in defense of liberty, the liberty of any human being, is no vice. Anytime anyone is enslaved or in any way deprived of his liberty, that person, as a human being, as far as I'm concerned he is justified to resort to whatever methods necessary to bring about his liberty again. [Applause][27]

This defense of liberty is strikingly similar to perhaps the best known of its kind in the English-speaking world. John Locke's "appeal to heaven," found in his Second Treatise of Government, is worth considering alongside Malcolm's right of last resort:

> The people have no other remedy in this, as in all other cases where they have no judge on Earth, but to appeal to heaven. For the rulers, in such attempts, exercising a power the people never put into their hands (who can never be supposed to consent, that any body should rule over them for their harm) do that, which they have not a right to do. And where the body of the people, or any single man, is deprived of their right, or is under the exercise of a power without right, and have no appeal on Earth, there they have a liberty to appeal to heaven, whenever they judge the Cause of sufficient moment.[28]

What Malcolm is really arguing is that extremism, like many other political concepts, is racially contingent. To get at the meaning of our common language—terms we presume to inherently understand—we must first remove ourselves from any vantage point of national or racial privilege. "When [the oppressed] say extremism, they don't mean what you do," Malcolm continued. "And when you say extremism, you don't mean what they do."[29] The barrier of racial superiority and inferiority inheres in these discussions and ultimately drowns out the ability to understand one another. As "the centers of power are changing" in the world, with Europe losing its hold on its colonies and prestige, Malcolm argues that a new language is emergent in the world—one predicated upon newly awakened and liberated peoples. "People in the past who weren't in a position to have a yardstick, or use a yardstick of their own, are using their own yardstick now," he explained at Oxford. "In the past, when the oppressor had one stick and the oppressed used that same stick, today the oppressed are sort of shaking the shackles and getting yardsticks of their own."[30] This understanding of the psychological nature of exploitation (and the related notion of psychological liberation from colonialism) would be picked up on and made central to more radical interpretations of global race relations by writers such as Frantz Fanon.[31] These early statements made by Malcolm at Oxford in some ways suggest there is far less tension between radical racial politics and notions of justice and other, more classical forms of liberal discourse.

"A good example is the Congo"

Nearly all of Malcolm's speeches and public statements leading up to Oxford touched on the developing political crisis in the former Belgian Congo. Immersed in a civil war after its independence from Belgium in 1960, the murder of the first elected prime minister, Patrice Lumumba, and the subsequent period of unrest, this mineral-rich African nation drew international condemnation and deep concern. The historic atrocities of the Belgians under King Leopold II in the Congo were now being revisited in a more modern, if not less horrible form. As the United States and its allies backed the new prime minister, Moise Tshombe, who favored continuing ties with Belgium and the West, Malcolm began to speak out more forcefully against the hypocrisy of "democratic" values in Africa and the false labeling of Congolese rebels in Stanleyville as "extremists." To put the rebels' plight in historic perspective, Malcolm employed none other than Mark Twain as a character witness for the people of the Congo—and their right to summon whatever opposition necessary to reverse a legacy of violence and terror in their country. Just one week before arriving in Oxford, Malcolm cited Twain's *King Leopold's Soliloquy* from 1905, demonstrating his intellectual range on the subject but also his skillful and novel use of white allies in the cause of racial justice:

> I was reading a book today by Mark Twain called King Leopold's Soliloquy, about Belgium. And it stated in there that when Belgium took over, the population of the Congo was something like 30 million and they reduced it to 15 million. If these aren't casualties, I don't know what casualties are. But while the Belgians were butchering the Congolese you'll find historians haven't recorded where there was all this concern, at that time, over the loss of human lives, as long as they were black lives. It seems that there wasn't much value placed upon them as was placed upon the handful of white hostages whose lives were threatened here earlier in the week.[32]

While his fellow panelists rejected Malcolm's (and ultimately Twain's) historical accounting, it nonetheless foreshadowed Malcolm's effective employ of white literary and intellectual icons to make his case. The tactic was a foreshadowing of Shakespeare's appearance at the very end of Malcolm's address at Oxford. Perhaps more important, Malcolm's case for extremism in the defense of liberty in the Congo was predicated on the people of the Congo's inherent humanity and self-worth. "The Congolese are just as humane, just as human, and just as intelligent as anybody else on this planet," Malcolm argued in this radio discussion. "And when they reflect this animosity and hostility I think anyone who goes over there and examines the facts [will] find out they're justified."[33]

The crisis in the Congo, like so much of international politics in the 1960s, was viewed almost exclusively through the lens of Cold War politics. As the political scientist Alvin Tillery Jr. has shown, even the black press in the United States was subject to revisionism in its accounts of Patrice Lumumba and the Congo, with the former prime minister depicted negatively by the black press 46 percent of the time (up from merely 3 percent) after his appeal for Soviet support.[34] Such media distortions were at the heart of Malcolm's Oxford speech. The Congo was but the latest and most effective example of well-constructed media bias, as he saw it. Indeed, the British Foreign Office observed both US and Soviet coverage of racial politics in the United States with a keen eye toward Cold War realpolitik. The substantive issue of black exploitation is almost ancillary to foreign policy concerns, as demonstrated by this letter filed by the British Embassy in June of 1963:

> Cloake reported that the Soviet press was playing up the racial troubles in the United States. The newspapers now carry daily reports on the subject, frequently embellished with prominent headlines and photographs of clashes between police and negroes.... [Soviet coverage states] the American way of life was based on racial inequality and the police state; while the Soviet Union was the first society of equal nations. Millions of negroes in America could no longer accept their lack of rights when in Africa hundreds of millions had broken their chains. Pious statements were being made in Washington, and it was possible that a few measures would be taken, but no deception by Washington politicians could obscure the obvious fact that they were not thinking of the genuine liquidation of racism.[35]

It is intriguing to consider how often the British Foreign Office saw an almost natural connection between African anticolonial movements and the struggle of American blacks for civil rights. Certainly, Malcolm was foremost among African Americans in making this claim. At Oxford, he did so beyond the more restrictive tenets of Black Nationalism or pan-Africanism. But first Malcolm was interested in unmasking the benevolent face of American and Western foreign policy in Africa:

They take American-trained—they take pilots that they say are American trained—and this automatically lends respectability to them, [*Laughter*] and then they will call them anti-Castro Cubans. And that's supposed to add to their respectability [*Laughter*] and eliminate the fact that they are dropping bombs on villages where they have no defense whatsoever against such planes, blowing to bits Black women—Congolese women, Congolese children, Congolese babies. This is extremism. But it is never referred to as extremism, because it is endorsed by the West, it's financed by America, it's made respectable by America, and that kind of extremism is never labeled as extremism.[36]

It is noteworthy that Malcolm moves in midstream from identifying the victims of such bombing campaigns as "black" to Congolese. While it is fundamental to his premise that black lives are not valued by the West and its press as equal to those of whites, he does not wish to make the reverse claim or make the racial identity of the dead preeminent. What is most important is that these atrocities are being committed against fellow human beings. Such violence or misleading reporting of these criminal acts is not beyond the pale of black humanity. Such falsifications "perhaps would have been practiced by others had they been in power," argues Malcolm, "but during recent centuries the West has been in power, they've created the images, and they've used these images quite skillfully."[37] In this new phase of Malcolm's political understanding, unrestrained power is the devil within humanity, not the blood that courses through the veins of whites.

While Malcolm's transformed racial cosmology failed to register among most members of the press, more avowedly moderate black voices in the United States found themselves torn over the situation in the Congo. The British Embassy in Washington closely followed the disagreements among civil rights leaders over the question of Congolese independence. Just two days before Malcolm confronted the issue of the indiscriminate bombing and use of force by the

United States and the Western powers in the Congo, the British Embassy in Washington cabled the newly elected prime minister, Harold Wilson, on the matter:

> As you may have seen from my letter of 1 December to Wilson, American negro leaders showed an increasing interest in American policy towards the Congo during the latter part of last year. At that time, it looked as if they might be starting something of a campaign to persuade the Administration to renounce its support for Tshombe. This would have been an embarrassment to the State Department, if not a major impediment to their policy. Against this background we were struck by the relative moderation of [civil rights leader James] Farmer's pronouncements about the Congo in the course of his African tour. The same moderation seems to have been displayed by other directors of the American Negro Leadership Conference on Africa who, together with Mr. Farmer, saw [Secretary of State Dean] Rusk for two hours on 3 March.... The negro leaders were reported by the press to have conceded to reporters after the meeting that the United States Government would have to continue to deal with Tshome. *It looks therefore, as if the State Department have this particular horse under reasonable control, at any rate for the moment.*[38]

Malcolm didn't need to see this bit of British intelligence to conclude that black leadership in the United States had become compromised on questions pertaining to Africa. The problem was twofold. African American leaders were called upon to demonstrate their loyalty to America by endorsing, or at a minimum remaining mum on, American foreign policy matters they deplored. By the same token, African heads of state, desperate for American dollars, were reluctant to adopt an openly anti-American position on any number of questions. The realities of domestic and foreign policy concerns made Malcolm's dream of bringing the United States up on violations of human rights with respect to African Americans all the more impractical. Malcolm was forced to conclude that "as long as you take money from America, you'll have only the external appearance of sovereignty."[39] Malcolm could not have come up with a better analogy than the British Embassy's. The bit in the proverbial horse under control—be it an American or African horse—was money.

The Smethwick Effect

As Malcolm wound his way through his address at Oxford, his reasoned endorsement of extremism had to serve as a conspicuous reminder, to many in his audience, of the recently passed national elections in Britain. Indeed, the city of Smethwick in England had become nearly synonymous with the issue of race—so much so that the town became a source of national attention well after the election itself. Malcolm visited the town just over a week before his murder. Its connection to American racial politics was not lost on Malcolm, or the candidates for office in the city. As *The Guardian* reported just prior to the election, the Labour candidate, Gordon Walker, facing an insurmountable surge by his opponent, Peter Griffiths, made the allusion directly. "[Griffiths] is one of the very few candidates in this election," said Walker, "who has come out openly for Senator Goldwater, on his side in the American election."[40] Unfortunately for Walker, his comparison was reviled, as he was heckled by cries of "rubbish" by his audience. In what proved to be the one bright spot for Conservatives in many respects on election night in England, the issues of immigration and racial assimilation were most salient.

By comparison, Lyndon Johnson's landslide defeat of Barry Goldwater suggested for many in the media the restoration, if not continuity, of American liberalism's "colorblind" character. Here were the American people in unison seeming to uniformly dismiss the extremism—indeed the racial extremism—of the far Right in exchange for inclusion and broadly shared rights. Conversely, throughout the UK, the idea of "Britishness" had come perilously close to being racialized. Harold Wilson and Labour's narrow victory over Sir Alec Douglas-Home and Conservatives was accompanied by overtly racial appeals and reductive definitions of English identity. Where the American election proved a decisive victory for progressive and antiracist forces, the British contest evoked the prospects of even more fragmented politics to come. Americans were putting race behind them. The British had it before them. Malcolm clearly saw such sentimentalizing and painless analysis of the American political scene as a gross distortion of reality in the aftermath of the elections of 1964. What's more, it missed the ways in which American and British politics enunciated a limited and hierarchical sense of citizenship, particularly as it related to racial and ethnic identity.

As discussed earlier, the consideration of race in British politics was introduced for the first time in 1964, by the political scientist David Butler, in his review of the national elections.[41]

Part of Malcolm's plan for his visit to Smethwick in 1965 included a failed attempt to meet with Peter Griffiths. In weighing the issue of race and immigration during his visit to Smethwick, Malcolm's recent experiences rushed to the fore of his analysis. "This problem," he told a correspondent for the *Times of London*, "makes the French, British and United States realize that whereas in the past the African revolution took place on the outside of the house, it is now on the inside of the house and it is causing concern."[42] Indeed, the changing color palette inside the debate hall at Oxford was proof positive that the 1960s represented a watershed moment in racial demographics and politics in the United Kingdom.

Of course, race's connection to immigration preceded the 1964 elections and the troubles of Smethwick. As Harold Macmillan recalled while serving in the last days of Winston Churchill's cabinet, the departing prime minister suggested the slogan "Keep England White" for the upcoming election campaign.[43] By the time Macmillan himself was serving as prime minister, he was immersed in efforts to get the Kennedy administration to accept Britain's "excess" black population from the West Indies.[44] Such racially based understandings of citizenship were a boon to Irish immigrants to England, for example, not altogether different than how "whiteness" was conferred upon the Irish in an America increasingly fraught with racially based divisions and hierarchies. When George Lincoln Rockwell, the American Nazi Party leader, was able to gain entry into England through Ireland in 1962, it only served to underscore how the Commonwealth Immigrants Act—passed to restrict in-migration to the UK from its Commonwealth countries—was deeply imbued with racial favoritism toward white members of the Commonwealth, or whites who sought entry through the proverbial "Irish back door," as it was called.[45] Labour Party and Opposition Leader Hugh Gaitskell called it "cruel and brutal anti-colour legislation."[46] One Tory representative explained the underlying fear of immigration during the Smethwick race in 1964 perhaps too well. "We have been out all morning with loudspeakers talking to the people," said the local Tory agent, a Mr. Charles Dickens, "and many of them have shaken Mr. Griffiths's hand and wished him well. The public knows the true position here about immigration. It is a matter of domestic hygiene and conduct, and that is very important in some parts of the town."[47]

The immigration issue had become so volatile in Smethwick that the BBC canceled a report on the "troubled" city weeks before the election. "We took a look at it," said a BBC spokesman, "and in the circumstances up there we thought we had better not do it."[48] By February, the BBC clearly thought things had calmed down sufficiently enough to cover Malcolm's visit. But during the election campaign and immediately thereafter, a great deal of caution was exercised by the network and candidates alike. Enoch Powell, who would go on to become most identified with the anti-immigration cause in England, and in a sense, was Goldwater's extremist counterpart across the Atlantic, was scheduled to visit Smethwick shortly before the election in October. His presence was seen as so inflammatory that he too canceled his appearance, ostensibly to attend a local council meeting. A conservative spokesman for the Midlands area perhaps protested too much when he assured *The Guardian* that there was "nothing sinister" about the cancellation.[49] *The Observer* more accurately opined that "it is widely assumed that Mr. Powell who is extremely hostile to bringing race into politics, was thought an embarrassment" to Griffiths.[50]

While Malcolm did not directly address immigration at Oxford, his racial readings into politics and prioritization of race with anti-colonial struggles around the world were no doubt unsettling to British political elites and media sources. Both major parties in the UK had agreed to de-escalate the racial question in their respective campaigns, making the topic a veritable taboo for candidates on both sides. As posters bearing the slogan "If you want a nigger neighbor, vote Labour" began to resurface days before the election, the level of obfuscation only heightened. "A Labour Party spokesman saw nothing in them to comment about," reported *The Guardian*. "Everybody always denies all knowledge of them," he said.[51] These evasions were an early form of overwrought postracialism, a way of avoiding uncomfortable discussions of race and its attendant issues. Because Malcolm saw the racial dynamic at the heart of American, and indeed much of the world's, injustice, he was an early apostate of postracialism, despite his religious conversion which imbued him with a new humanism. When the killing of white hostages was raised at Oxford, Malcolm rejected the easiness of "colorblindness" while making his case for extremism in the defense of liberty:

> I don't encourage any acts of murder, nor do I glorify in anybody's death, but I do think that when the white public uses its press to magnify the fact that there are the lives of white hostages at stake—they don't say "hostages," every paper says "white hostages"—they give me the impression that they attach more importance to a white hostage and a white death than they do the death of a human being despite the color of his skin. [Applause]....I think that white people are making the mistake—and if they read their

own newspapers, they will have to agree—that they, in clear-cut language, make a distinction between the type of dying according to the color of the skin. And when you begin to think in terms of death being death, no matter what type of human being it is, then we will all probably be able to sit down as human beings and get rid of this extremism and moderation. But as long as the situation exists as it is, we're going to need some extremism, and I think some of you will need some moderation too.[52]

It is important to remember, as Kathleen Paul noted in her study of race and British citizenship, that Enoch Powell's views on immigration, while often seen as extreme, fell within the mainstream of British conceptions of national identity. This perspective includes Powell's striking statement that the "West Indian or Indian does not, by being born in England, become an Englishman. In law he becomes a United Kingdom citizen by birth; in fact he is a West Indian or an Asian still."[53] Malcolm saw this reality as part of the African American experience—an internal colony perspective increasingly employed by black scholars in the United States in the 1960s and 1970s. In point of fact, Malcolm saw "American" identity for blacks in the United States as tenuous at best. Malcolm's response to all forms of Powellism—be they domestic or otherwise—was the logical extension of the American Negro's situation in the United States. "Being born here in America doesn't make you an American," he often argued. "Why, if birth made you an America, you wouldn't need any legislation, you wouldn't need any amendments to the Constitution, you wouldn't be faced with civil-rights filibustering in Washington, D.C., right now."[54] For his analysis, Malcolm was upbraided by the BBC's hosts for exaggerating the severity of race relations in the United States. "I'm speaking as a Black man from America," Malcolm argued during his talk, "which is a racist society. No matter how much you hear it talk about democracy, it's as racist as South Africa or as racist as Portugal, or as racist as any other racialist society on this earth."[55] "That was Malcolm X and his picture of the United States," one of the BBC hosts commented after Malcolm finished his remarks, "which I think won't be one we will necessarily find here." Another analyst went further, calling Malcolm's linkage of American racial policies with those of South Africa a "grotesque misrepresentation."[56]

In his advocacy of extremism in the defense of liberty, Malcolm paid careful attention to his own image and sought to restore a sense of humanity to his persona, as he attempted with his opening quip. Many of his efforts in this regard were linked to his analysis of the press and the role of the media in creating caricatures that satisfy powerful interests. The concluding remarks of the BBC broadcast that evening stand as monuments to the difficulty he had in recasting his public image, particularly in the last year of his life. Demolishing this caricature was part of Malcolm's objective at Oxford, where he hoped a less filtered presentation would augur well for his efforts to internationalize the struggle for racial justice for African Americans. His preparatory notes for Oxford were not very different from the ones used for the last speeches of his life. They emphasized "imagery" and "my own distorted image" repeatedly. Other notes in his diary refer to the "Science of Imagery: skillful use of press" and "Victims made to appear as criminals."[57] Understanding the difficulty of making extremism a legitimate tool in the quest for justice given his own image as an extremist, Malcolm adopted a number of rhetorical tools at Oxford that served to draw him closer to his audience. As he did with his repetitive "cutting" technique, Malcolm also employed a term at Oxford that embellished his rebuke of America's mistreatment of its black citizens—while simultaneously making his logic less alien to his critics.

Racialism and Rhetoric

Midway through his address, Malcolm sought to enlist whites in the cause of extremism in the defense of liberty for African Americans.

The effort was undertaken with Malcolm's characteristically fiery delivery; but it ended with an often underestimated dimension of his oratorical skill—humor:

> I live in America where there are only 22 million Blacks against probably 160 million whites. One of the reasons that I'm in no way reluctant or hesitant to do whatever is necessary to see that Black people do something to protect themselves: I honestly believe that the day that they do, many whites will have more respect for them. And there will be more whites on their side than are now on their side with this little wishy-washy "love-thy-enemy" approach that they've been using up to now. And if I'm wrong, then you are racialists. [*Laughter and applause*][58]

Malcolm pauses a beat before delivering the last line of this sequence. It is as if he senses the audience tightening, reacting to his rejection of Christian passivism. And in an instant, as if to suggest he knows his audience better than they know themselves, he offers the argument that at once acquits them while making them his radical allies. You as whites know passivism has its limits, he reasons; why not openly acknowledge this when the cause is *black* freedom? If you do, Malcolm suggests, you will be disproving all I had previously thought of you. It is an ingenious and, in a sense, rather heady line of attack. It is made all the more subtle by Malcolm's use of the term "racialists." In the context of the overall Oxford address, Malcolm's language here must be carefully scrutinized.

The use of the term "racialism" or its variants had to strike those familiar with Malcolm's addresses back in the States as odd. There doesn't appear to be a single instance where the word was ever used by Malcolm before an American audience. Why now, and why at Oxford? To start, the Oxford English Dictionary describes racialism as a simple extension of the term "racism."[59] But this doesn't quite hold true historically, as it seems "racialism" held different meanings, particularly in the early part of the twentieth century, when it began to be widely used. At times, racialism suggested an acceptance of racial distinctions without the accompanying belief in racially inferior or superior beings. The philosopher Kwame Anthony Appiah has framed this perspective well, arguing that racialists believe that "there are heritable characteristics, possessed by members of our species, which allow us to divide them into a small set of races, in such a way that all the members of these races share certain traits and tendencies with each other that they do not share with members of any other race."[60] In this vein, "racialism" conveys the same reductionist character that "racism" holds. The difference is that racialism's history has not always employed the term to connote inferiority or superiority upon particular groups. As Appiah notes, W. E. B. Du Bois and other black intellectuals found the idea of racialism laudable in the sense of ascribing to blacks their own racial "gifting." Nevertheless, its use in more recent times has been controversial, as people of color have argued that the term is a clever dodge of the charge of racism, allowing racists to have their cake and eat it too.

The earliest uses of the term "racialism" are employed in association with British imperialism and, later, the rise of Nazism in Germany.[61] The word fell into disuse after the Second World War and then reappeared in books at greater rates during decolonization and the American civil rights movement. The term has since fallen into disfavor, returning to pre–World War II levels.[62] At Oxford, Malcolm goes on to use the term "racialism" or "racialist" some eleven times. His use of the word clearly places him in an international context; he is no longer speaking American English. By eschewing "racism" for "racialism," Malcolm is communicating more directly with an Anglo and postcolonial audience that know that word best. Given that he does not use it in the States and it does not seem to appear anywhere in his personal writings, it may be presumed that this was a term he picked up in his travels abroad, most likely in the UK. He clearly found it of great use at Oxford:

> "I don't believe in any form of racialism."
> "And if I am wrong, then you are racialists."
> "Ten of the sixteen senatorial committees are in the hands of southern racialists."
> "The racialist never understands the nonviolent language."

These are but a handful of the times Malcolm uses the term at Oxford. In his understanding of rhetoric, Malcolm recognized that his use of the term "racist" or "racism" in England would only render his critique all the more foreign. His *Americanness* in this sense would be an ironic betrayal of his efforts to transcend political boundaries in making his case on the behalf of African Americans and Africans in Europe. Ever the traveler, the perennially displaced person in a lifetime of moves and reinventions, Malcolm's language becomes as evolved as the man. The two are indeed inseparable.

In similar fashion, Malcolm utilizes a rhetorical device throughout his speech at Oxford that effectively invites his audience into his worldview. Early in his address, Malcolm argues that "the centers of power are changing" and that in this transforming world clinging to outdated understandings and suppositions simply won't do. Malcolm makes US foreign policy the object lesson of this premise:

> They'll take a person who's the victim of the crime and make it appear he's the criminal, and they'll take the criminal and make it appear he's the victim of the crime.[63]

This form of chiastic rhetoric, sometimes referred to as a verbal "reversible raincoat," has a long and influential history, ranging from biblical scripture to Dante to John F. Kennedy ("ask not what your country can do for you").

Perhaps Malcolm's most widely quoted chiastic phrase was

⎰ We didn't land on Plymouth Rock;
⎱ Plymouth Rock landed on us.[64]

At Oxford, Malcolm employs chiasmus, or the redirecting of the second part of an expression back to the first, on several occasions. He begins with his initial line about the meaning of extremism. He then uses it to explain how American-financed bombing of Congolese "women and children" is "extremism in defense of liberty for the wrong type of people."[65] The turn of phrase is also used to categorize American "racialism" in the same vein as that of Portugal or South Africa.

> South Africa preaches separation and practices separation;
> America preaches integration and practices segregation.
> This is the only difference.
> They don't practice what they preach,
> whereas South Africa preaches and practices the same thing.[66]

The simple, biting logic of Malcolm draws frequent applause throughout his presentation, but it is not unchallenged. In response to a question from the audience thrust at him about the killings in the Congo, Malcolm argued that the killing of missionaries by the Congolese was an act of war, and no different than similar or more extensive acts of killing by the Allies during the Second World War. "When you call it war, then anybody that dies, they die a death that is justified," he says to groans and shouts from the audience.[67] From this difficult point, Malcolm pivots and argues that these killings in the Congo only took place after "the paratroopers came in." His statement is applauded if not universally agreed to—and then he builds upon an Augustinian-styled just war theory, challenging his audience to view the killing of black Congolese with equal sorrow as they view the white hostages of Stanleyville. Malcolm's unasked but implied question is: Why do you cry for whites who are dying but not for Africans? Malcolm seems to provide the answer—it is not the inherent racism or evil of whites, but rather the result of a media culture that sustains a partial and racist narrative.

> The powers that be use the press to give the devil an angelic image and give the image of the devil to the one who's really angelic.[68]

Interestingly, Malcolm invokes the angelic/demonic binary several times at Oxford, drawing applause from the audience on two occasions. Despite leaving behind the racially dependent theology of the Nation of Islam, Malcolm continues to employ the "devil" in his rhetoric. But at Oxford, as it had been for nearly all of 1964, it was a response to a condition or type of individual rather than an inherited characteristic of whites. Malcolm seems to stress this as he mocks his own "devilish" image by recounting his dinner with a female student at Oxford who was "searching for his horns."[69] While playfully chiding the audience for thinking something untoward was going on between him and the young coed, Malcolm returns to how he, like other victims of oppression, becomes popularly branded as an "extremist." Throwing a line to his otherwise fiercely engaged audience, Malcolm excoriated the press with the aplomb of a man not in his own country. "Not so much your press," he said with a smile, "but the American press, which has tricked your press into repeating what they have invented" [*Laughter and applause*]. Malcolm did not win every convert to his cause at Oxford, but his defense of extremism and overall skill as a debater did win its share of plaudits. "Malcolm X, whose appearance in the debate was a comparative sensation," wrote the British television critic Gerald Larner, "was very fluent and, speaking in defence of extremism, was himself extreme—perhaps too extreme, to be persuasive, *but an experience.*"[70]

Such grudging respect was perhaps all Malcolm could hope for from the press. What he ultimately wanted was a hearing before the court of public opinion, in front of the largest audience he could find. He found much, if not all of it, at Oxford. But what of "liberty?" As the BBC and British press had focused upon Goldwater's "extremism" line, the subject of the motion's first proposition had all but been forgotten. "Extremism in the defense of liberty is no vice," it was said. But had anyone considered precisely what liberty meant? Malcolm's own personal discovery of liberty in 1964 and his efforts to find a political solution to the question of racial liberation would find a surprising home in his address at Oxford.

Chapter 3

Liberty: "Please forward by any means necessary"

In the middle of May of 1964, just weeks after his pilgrimage to Mecca, Malcolm X's Harlem office began mass producing a most unusual piece of correspondence. It was a form letter intending to reach out to those individuals and organizations that Malcolm had in some way alienated, ridiculed, or condemned in years past. The letters were mailed to stalwarts of the civil rights movement—men such as John Lewis, chairman of the Student Nonviolent Coordinating Committee, James Farmer of the Congress of Racial Equality, Whitney Young of the National Urban League, A. Philip Randolph of the Brotherhood of Sleeping Car Porters, Roy Wilkins of the NAACP—and another was addressed to the headquarters of the Southern Christian Leadership Conference in Atlanta, and one "Reverend Dr. Martin Luther King."[1] These were all members of what Malcolm had mockingly dubbed "The Big Six"—leaders of the most respected civil rights organizations in America, whose nonviolent approached Malcolm had frequently attacked.[2] None but Farmer had ever agreed to debate or make a formal appearance with Malcolm. Despite having denounced him as an "almost white man" in early 1963 for having married a white woman, Malcolm had developed deep respect for Farmer.[3] By late 1964, he had met with Farmer personally, including a short meeting with Farmer's wife.[4] Malcolm was now in the business of reconciliation and sought to influence, rather than berate, others with his politics. Writing to Maya Angelou in Ghana in January of 1965 just one month before his assassination,

he asked her to seek out Farmer, who was visiting the African nation
in the near future:

> I hope that you will get this letter before James Farmer arrives. The
> Afro-American community there should not shun him but should
> encircle him and make sure that he is exposed to the right kind of
> thinking. I hope he has an opportunity to meet Mr. [David] Du
> Bois and also the President. Please convey that message...for me
> so that he will be exposed to the most undiluted African thinking.[5]

The American embassy in Ghana ultimately saw Farmer's visit
as "undoing in part the damage caused by two Malcolm X visits."
Malcolm's murder in February of 1965 had the effect of cutting short
some of the more radical efforts of African American organizations
in Africa.[6] Malcolm's unusual form letter reflected the breadth of
the struggle he now deemed necessary to effectuate change, both at
home and abroad. "We have no restrictions of religious ties, political preferences nor organizational leanings of those who wish to
participate with us," read the statement. Knowing how his remarks
must have stung over the years, Malcolm's letter also offered a promise. "Minister Malcolm has also made public his intentions not to
attack any person or organization that is engaged in the struggle. He
also asks forgiveness for the unkind things that he has said in the
past."[7] Malcolm's religious and political liberation from the Nation
of Islam's orthodoxy was but the first step in recasting his role in the
black liberation movement of the time. Malcolm also understood
that he had to mend fences with those with whom he disagreed, if
his involvement was to have real significance. While Malcolm offered
no apologies at Oxford for his past beliefs and criticisms of civil
rights organizations, he did hope to connect his personal spiritual
liberation to the politics of black freedom. The path that Malcolm
took to Oxford, one which led him to declare in the debate hall, "I
for one will join in with anyone, I don't care what color you are,"
was not an easy one. Redefining politics meant redefining Malcolm's

own identity. This process began as early as March of 1964 and his break from the Nation of Islam. At Oxford, he would have a little over thirty minutes to meld these twin senses of liberty before millions of viewers around the world.

The Ides of March and Beyond

"I am a Muslim," Malcolm said only three minutes into his address at Oxford. "If there is something wrong with that, then I stand condemned." Fifteen minutes later Malcolm reminded his audience in the debate hall and around the world of his religious affiliation. "As I said earlier, in my conclusion, I'm a Muslim," he repeated. "I believe in Allah, I believe in Muhammad, I believe in all of the prophets. I believe in fasting, prayer, charity, and that which is incumbent upon a Muslim to fulfill in order to be a Muslim."[8] Aside from Tariq Ali's burst of applause at the first declaration of Malcolm's faith—something that drew laughter from the audience—there was a stony and respectful silence in the debate hall at Oxford. While Malcolm's religion was employed during the debate to establish his moderation—a point to be taken up in the next chapter—it was also a personal characteristic offered to exemplify his freedom from the religious orthodoxy of the Nation of Islam. Because Malcolm had entertained classical notions of his bond with Elijah Muhammad—he was Aristotle to Elijah's Socrates, as he wrote in his *Autobiography*—the break with the NOI was both personal and epic.[9] But once Malcolm was told by James Shabazz, his future secretary with the Muslim Mosque, Incorporated, that his departure from the organization was tantamount to his death, Malcolm understood that the clock of mortality was ticking. "Look brother," Shabazz told Malcolm, "you were seen in favor by Mr. Muhammad. And I hope you will return to his favor. [But] no, you're not going back in the Nation. People are talking about killing you."[10] Malcolm was tragically placed in the position of Socrates, however, telling his friends that he could not choose to remain in exile abroad; he was to take his hemlock in America's black Athens—Harlem.[11]

While Malcolm had to have seen "white" Muslims in his travels abroad in 1959, one which included a visit to the United Arab Republic, his hajj journey was undertaken under his own religious and political leadership. Malcolm was free not only to deduce, but to articulate, his own vision of racial and religious identity's meaning on both a personal and a universal level. In his diary, Malcolm described the symbiotic relationship between his religious awakening and the possibilities for racial brotherhood:

> Visit cockpit, 1st time in my life (all Egyptian pilots) on my way to Mecca. Honor and respect—I felt so humble. Never in America had I received such respect + honor as here in the Muslim world, just upon learning I am a Muslim. People: white, black, brown, red [and] yellow—all act alike as one, as *Bros*. People with blue eyes + blonde hair, bowing in complete submission to Allah, beside those with black skin + kinky hair. As they give the *same* honor to the same God, they in turn give some (equal) honor to each other.[12]

Malcolm's hajj journey naturally led him to reflect upon his earlier visit to the Middle East and what might have been. "I had deferred going [to Mecca] in '59," he wrote during his pilgrimage five years later, "because my respect and devotion to [the Honorable Elijah Muhammad] made me not want to go there ahead of him."[13] From the mundane to the sublime, Malcolm's conversion to Orthodox Islam enlivened in him a broader hopefulness for humanity, and specifically relations between blacks and whites, than was previously conceivable. Nothing surpassed his excitement about Islam's potential to transcend racial and socioeconomic differences during the hajj. "People," he jotted down parenthetically, "all snore in the same language—smile." Such musings did not mean Malcolm was succumbing to Pollyannaish views on race. Retaining his fierce devotion to a more militant form of politics, his changed worldview became more about encompassing, rather than cordoning off, potential allies in the struggle for racial justice.

After Oxford, a letter would be delivered by airmail to Malcolm's Harlem office. Addressed to "Mr. Malcolm X" and the "Organization for Afro-American Unity, Harlem, New York City, U.S.A." without so much as a zip code, the author almost imploringly included on the upper left corner a winking plea: "PLEASE FORWARD BY ANY MEANS NECESSARY." The writer was a young woman named Sandra M. Devoto of Sheffield, England. She had heard Malcolm speak in Sheffield after his brief stint there and in Manchester, the day after the Oxford talk. Dated December 5, the day after his departure from the UK, the letter is worth reprinting here in its entirety, as it conveys how Malcolm's own personal liberation embodied great potential for a more radical politics to emerge within the context of multiracial communities in the West:

Dear Malcolm X,

I am the girl in the turquoise sweater, pearl necklace, and black skirt who shook hands with you saying I agreed with everything you said. Believe me, I really mean it.

Politically I hold no firm views, can be swayed, see both sides of the question. Religiously also I can see all good and bad points in all faiths. There are only two things in which I take a sure and steadfast stand, I am against, with no reservations whatever, Prejudice, especially racial or colour prejudice and Hypocrisy. To me, these are the worst sins and the greatest trouble causes in the world today. I hope you don't dismiss this letter as stupid, there are so many things I would like to say, but alas, am not as articulate as I would like to be.

If only there was something I could do to help, however, I don't know what you would feel or do about an Anglo-Italian, female agnostic who doesn't see what she can do anyway. I know you have a great sense of humour, so am sure you will at least have a laugh!

All of us here will I am sure, follow your progress with great hope and enthusiasm. I certainly hope that you will visit this country and come to Sheffield again in the near future, though of course I realize that your work lies in the "United" States. Please let me know if there is anything I can do to help as I feel so impotent sitting here talking and discussing the problem but never being able to do anything constructive.

I shall never forget meeting you,

> Yours sincerely,
> Salaam,
> Sandra M. Devoto (Miss)[14]

Malcolm did indeed return to England in February of 1965. And while there is no indication he ever met or responded to Sandra Devoto, we can discern in her letter the outlines of a plausible new constituency for Malcolm's post-Meccan message—the one he best articulated at Oxford. It is one that would attract large, disaffected segments of white British society: it would be disproportionately female; it would in all likelihood be made up of those without committed religious affiliations or beliefs; and it would likewise conceivably be composed of white ethnics whose place in British society remained uncertain. Such an ensemble of white allies was impermissible in Malcolm's former political and theological cosmology. In the *Autobiography*, Malcolm told of his later regret for telling a "blonde New England co-ed" that there was nothing she could do to help change society.[15] Malcolm's reversal was not built upon an imagined disappearance of white racism or some hoped-for rejection of America or the world's conception of white supremacy. Malcolm's transformation and subsequent embrace of whites was rooted in the acknowledgment that human capacity for struggle—to identify with the oppressed—is not bounded by color. More to the point, before moving on to Malcolm's personal liberation and its connection to the global struggle for independence movements in Africa and around the world, it is important to consider how such a dramatic departure in Malcolm's thinking also was tied to certain fundamental beliefs which he would not give up—at Oxford or anyplace else.

Remaining X

When Malcolm returned from his hajj in May of 1964, one of the most striking changes he announced to the world was his new name. El-Hajj Malik El-Shabazz was at once familiar and curious to those versed in Islamic custom. The honorific term "El Hajj" was bestowed upon Malcolm as someone who had completed the prescribed pilgrimage to Islam's holiest city. This was hardly novel; what was notable was that Malcolm elected to keep the name Malik El-Shabazz—the one given to him by Elijah Muhammad—and widely used by him as far back as 1957.[16] As C. Eric Lincoln explained in his classic study of the Nation of Islam, the term "Shabazz," however, was one with a very specific attachment to the organization's racial cosmology:

> The so-called Negro in America is a blood-descendant of the Original Man. "Who is better knowing of whom we are than God Himself? He has declared that we are descendants of the Asian Black Nation and of the tribe of Shabazz," which "came with the earth" when a great explosion divided the earth and the moon "sixty-six trillion years ago." The tribe of Shabazz was the first to explore the planet and discover the choicest parts in which to live....Elijah Muhammad and his followers have accepted the task of teaching the so-called Negroes that they are of the tribe of Shabazz and, therefore, "Original."[17]

Often referred to as "the Lost and Found" Nation of Islam, African Americans represented a mythical connection to this origin of man narrative in NOI theology. The question is, given his efforts to attain credibility as an Orthodox Muslim, why would Malcolm retain the surname "Shabazz?" Moreover, why would he remain "X?"

The latter question is easier to answer as Malcolm saw his "X" as a connection to the unknown familial legacies of so many African Americans.[18] But beyond its historical significance, Malcolm's X was a political statement. "Will you now use Shabazz and drop 'X'?" Malcolm was asked at a press conference upon his return to New York after making the hajj. "I will probably continue to use Malcolm X… as long as the situation that produced it exists," he said, chuckling. "You don't feel that Shabazz takes the place of X?" he was further pressed. "My going to Mecca and going into the Muslim world, into the African world and being recognized and accepted as a Muslim and as a brother, may solve the problem for me personally," Malcolm explained, "but I personally feel that my personal problem is never solved as long as the problem is not solved for all of our people in this country. So I will remain 'Malcolm X' as long as [there's] the need to struggle and protest and fight against the injustices that our people are involved in, in this country."[19] Two weeks before his arrival at Oxford, the BBC broadcast an earlier interview with Malcolm, again, raising the question of his "true" name. The interviewer, Cliff Michelmore, from the evening program *Tonight*, with some 7 million viewers around the world, began his short talk with Malcolm by asking him to "help clear up the question of your name":

MICHELMORE: Was it [your name] in fact Malcolm Little?
MALCOLM X: I don't think it was "in fact," if it was in fact, I would have let it remain. "Little" was the name of the man who formerly owned my grandfather as a slave, so I gave it back. (*Smiling*)[20]

Malcolm's ongoing sparring sessions over the continued use of his "X" reflected his acknowledgment of the distance between an idealized (and ahistorical) world often suggested by his questioners and the present realities of racial injustice he wished to highlight. For Malcolm, his personal liberation as an individual ought not to lead to the dissolution, but rather, the affirmation of one's connection to the struggle for racial justice. This is why at Oxford he unsurprisingly rejected both the lure of "colorblindness" as well as the exclusivity of Black Nationalism. As for "Shabazz," it seems as though Malcolm's personal connections to both the NOI's past and the Honorable Elijah Muhammad were too strong to sever all at once. Malcolm had, after all, named one of his daughters—Ilyasah Shabazz—after Elijah Muhammad, and the better part of his adult life was influenced by the teachings of the man he at one time deemed to be the Messenger of Allah. All the same, less than two weeks after announcing his official split with the Nation of Islam, Malcolm made a sobering amendment to his financial deal with the literary agency Paul R. Reynolds & Son. Reynolds, who had represented such luminaries as Richard Wright and the estate of Henry and William James, was now to "direct all proceeds" to the Muslim Mosque, Incorporated, the organization he founded, instead of to the NOI headquarters in Chicago.[21] Malcolm's revised arrangement of terms—signed by both him and his wife, for her "signature verification"—also made clear that "In the event of my death, I wish all proceeds to be made payable to my wife, Mrs. Betty X. Little."[22]

As Malcolm passionately defended the continual employment of his "X" in the face of Humphry Berkeley's efforts to trivialize the matter altogether during the Oxford debate, he was at the same time being threatened to give up his adopted iconic surname by the organization he once represented. In "An Open Letter to Malcolm Little" the NOI issued a scathing letter from the office of Mosque Number 7 in Harlem, calling upon Malcolm to "Stop Using 'X'":

Hypocrite, You are not with The Honorable Elijah Muhammad and you have proven yourself to be 100% against him and his followers. Then we ask you, why are you still carrying The Honorable Elijah Muhammad's name?? Why are you still using the "X" since you don't believe in our Saviour Master W.D. Fard? Why are you still using the Name "Shabazz" since you don't believe in The

Honorable Elijah Muhammad?? How come you still refer to your-self as "MALIK EL SHABAZZ" or MALCOLM X, since you have turned your back on the TRUTH that The Honorable Elijah Muhammad has given to the so-called Negro? Since you have turned away from the religion and the Nation of Islam...then we say..."HYPOCRITE GIVE UP THE X"..."HYPOCRITE GIVE UP SHABAZZ!" You are in possession of another man's property. The names belong to Allah and The Honorable Elijah Muhammad!!!! But if you give up those HOLY NAMES, where can you turn? Where will you go?...You have to go back to being LITTLE or RED!!!![23]

While representing an at once fearsome, and at times, inchoate set of arguments, the letter's underlying point was hardly irrational. Malcolm's newfound religious orthodoxy would seem to harbor little value for the nomenclature of NOI ideology. And yet Malcolm's willful hold and defense of his name at Oxford and throughout the last months of his life presaged a truth made popular by perhaps millions of youth in both the United States and throughout the world after his death. Malcolm's X had become something more than what the Nation of Islam taught or what Malcolm himself employed. It was to become, in time, the hammer and sickle of defiance against racially based black suffering throughout the world.[24] And Malcolm had an instinctive desire to go to his grave with it.

There is some degree of historic irony in Malcolm fighting to retain his adopted name in this way. Many African Americans went through the process of changing their names after slavery, some-times by simply adopting or dropping a single letter from their slave master's inherited name. Indeed, even while enslaved, blacks often called one another by different names once out of earshot of their masters.[25] Others, upon emancipation, changed their names entirely, creating wholly new personas at times, to differentiate the transition from slavery to freedom. As Nell Irvin Painter points out, Isabella Van Wagener's becoming Sojourner Truth was a response to the promptings of "The Holy Spirit" as much as it was a reflection of her connection to her enduring state of "homelessness."[26] Similarly, Richard Allen, founder of the African Methodist Episcopal Church and the Free African Society in Philadelphia in the late eighteenth century, adopted his last name, in what his biographer Richard S. Newman has called "the first act of self-possession in his life."[27] Perhaps the most well-known figure to adopt a new identity in this manner was one Frederick Augustus Washington Bailey, who became Frederick Douglass in 1838. Edward J. Blum among others has seen these personal affirmations of rediscovered self as integral to broader explorations of black identity. Whether it was Allen, Truth, Douglass, or Malcolm X, each used a personal autobiographical narrative to "carve out a space for African American religious, individual, and collective expression."[28]

For Malcolm, his transformation represented a kind of double freedom—becoming X was a freedom from white identity and familial ties. Becoming *El-Hajj Malik El-Shabazz* was a freedom from organizational orthodoxy within the NOI and its deviation from acceptable Islamic teachings. And yet, by remaining X and *Malik El-Shabazz*, Malcolm was holding on to two visions of himself and his politics. He was linking himself to the black diaspora in the "Western Hemisphere," as he responded to Berkeley at Oxford; and he was forging ties to the broader *Dar al-Islam*—the Muslim world that he had already joined to great personal satisfaction. In reaching out in this way, Malcolm also sought to project himself as someone whose extremism was within the bounds of moral conduct—despite whatever images of himself were formed in the minds of his worldwide audience.

"By any means necessary"

At Oxford, Malcolm employed three iterations of his iconic phrase "by any means necessary." Part of the allure of the expression has been its catch-all quality. The great and (for some) disturbing ambiguity of the line is premised upon its generic lack of qualification.

What, exactly, is necessary? The absence of a subject invites specu-
lation about not only Malcolm's intent, but the listener's own fears,
doubts, and expectations. Malcolm's implication is that the struggle
for racial justice for African Americans may be won by any act that
is essential to bringing about their liberty. By reducing Malcolm to
this phrase, there has been a tendency to de-emphasize the word
"necessary" or the essentialist quality of the expression. If it is unnec-
essary, the action in question ought not to be taken—whatever its
nature. Yet when heard not only by whites, but also by blacks, many
took the expression as an open call to violence. And while Malcolm
didn't reject this possibility—one he deemed appropriate for all
human beings denied their fundamental rights—he certainly used
the phrase as a mirror to hold up to his audience as a kind of gauge
of their own racial sensibilities. If whites feared the expression, they
did not genuinely believe in the equality of black people; if blacks
feared it, they were in abject denial of their own humanity. In the
same BBC interview with *Tonight*, broadcast two weeks before the
Oxford debate, Malcolm identified the expression as central to his
political objectives:

MICHELMORE: The Black Muslim policy as I was saying was com-
    pletely separatist. They wanted this separate state within the United
    States. Now, as I understand it you don't. The policy of your group
    is now that you don't. How do you want, what do you want?

MALCOLM X: Well, number one, there are two groups of us now,
    that is those who broke away have formed into two groups, one
    which is religious and based upon the orthodox Islamic teach-
    ing, and the other is non-religious and the name of it is the
    Organization of Afro-American Unity, and we want to be rec-
    ognized and respected as human beings and we have a motto
    which tells somewhat how we intend to bring it about, our
    motto is "by any means necessary." By whatever means is nec-
    essary to bring about complete respect and recognition of the
    twenty-two million black people in America, as human beings,
    that's what we are for, that's what we're dedicated to.

MICHELMORE: "By any means?" By *any* means?

MALCOLM X: By any means.

MICHELMORE: A bloodbath?

MALCOLM X: Well I think as deplorable as the word bloodbath may sound, I think the condition that Negroes in America have already experienced in America, for too long, is just as deplorable and if it takes something that deplorable to remove this other deplorable condition, I think it is justified.

Malcolm instinctively employed the "necessary" clause at Oxford to beat back the notion that his "extremism" was somehow of an unethical or depraved stripe. Malcolm makes first use of the expression early in his address, to establish the humanitarian basis of what effectively amounts to the right to revolution:

Anytime anyone is enslaved or in any way deprived of his liberty, that person, as a human being, as far as I'm concerned he is justified to resort to whatever methods necessary to bring about his liberty again.[29]

He then proceeded to apply the expression to the failure of government to provide its most basic protections for its citizens—in this case, those in the United States fighting for racial equality, such as the "three civil rights workers murdered [Goodman, Schwerner, and Chaney] in cold blood." Jan Carew, the founder of the black British publication *Magnet*, and a friend of Malcolm's, recalled how at the London School of Economics ten weeks later, during this portion of the speech, there was a "subdued anger" in Malcolm's voice while "his eyes glittered like diamonds" as he recalled the infamous murders.[30] At Oxford, Malcolm's voice rose in intensity as he continued this line of argument:

So my contention is that whenever a people come to the conclusion that the government which they have supported proves itself unwilling or proves itself unable to protect our lives and protect our property because we have the wrong color skin, we are not human beings unless we ourselves band together and do whatever, however, whenever is necessary to see that our lives and our property are protected.[31]

Finally, after citing the brutal treatment against blacks by the American state ("We are the ones who have our skulls crushed, not by the Ku Klux Klan but by *policemen*"), Malcolm closes this argument by taking the ineffectuality of the law into account:

> Well, any time you live in a society supposedly based upon law, and it doesn't enforce its own law because the color of a man's skin happens to be wrong, then I say those people are justified to resort to any means necessary to bring about justice where the government can't give them justice. [*Applause*][32]

It's worth pointing out that for Malcolm, violence was but one, and indeed a last, means for attaining justice. As he had made clear in his "The Ballot or the Bullet" speech in late 1963, there were political pathways to liberty as he saw it, dwindling though they were. The critical point was that most whites could not accept that blacks were entitled to the same Jeffersonian right to revolution as they were. The point was made plain by Malcolm in one of the more humorous moments during the debate. In the middle of his talk, Malcolm returned to his critique of the Western press and its effort to portray those with an "uncompromising attitude against the injustices" experienced by African Americans as "rabble-rousers" or as irrational. At this moment, Malcolm is interrupted.

INTERJECTION: I wonder whether you'd consider that you have seen me projected, rather successfully, a quite unpleasant image of a "type."

MALCOLM X: It depends on which angle—[protests from audience] No, let the gentleman bring out his point. It depends on which angle you look at it, sir. I'm not—I never try and hide what I am. If—

SAME PERSON: I'm referring to more your treatment of the previous speaker.

MALCOLM X: You're referring to my treatment of the previous speaker? [Laughter and applause] You make my point, [Laughter] that as long as a white man does it, it's all right. A Black man is supposed to have no feelings. [Applause] So when a Black man strikes back, he's an extremist. He's supposed to sit passively and have no feelings, be nonviolent, and love his enemy. No matter what kind of attack, be it verbal or otherwise, he's supposed to take it. But if he stands up and in any way tries to defend himself, [Malcolm laughs] then he's an extremist [Laughter and applause].[33]

When listening to the exchange, it seems as though perhaps Humphry Berkeley was interjecting on his own behalf. Given Malcolm's cutting attacks on him earlier in the debate ("that type"), it would be understandable, but read more closely, and with the advantage of Malcolm's retort partly covered during the BBC broadcast, we can discern that in all probability this is someone other than Berkeley coming to his defense. Malcolm's witty response did draw smiles and warm applause from the audience, which less than thirty minutes before had heard Berkeley's assault upon Malcolm, including the attack upon his name. At this moment of the exchange, the BBC camera panned from Malcolm to Tariq Ali, beside himself with joy, clapping enthusiastically, while laughing along with others in the hall. To Ali's left, Hugh MacDiarmid sat impassively, absorbing it all in his usual, cerebral fashion.[34] Yet Malcolm clearly made an impression upon him. Recalling the debate a year later in his memoir, in a chapter entitled "My Friends," MacDiarmid remembered Malcolm as "a brilliant speaker and to my mind an extremely able and attractive personality."[35] For his part, Malcolm would recall MacDiarmid fondly, as he reflected upon MacDiarmid's channeling of the English poet William Blake at Oxford. "The road to excess leads to the palace of wisdom," MacDiarmid had quoted Blake, during his speech supporting the motion on extremism at Oxford. "If only I had the time to read everything I should read!" Malcolm lamented, recalling MacDiarmid's line. "Blake sounds interesting."[36]

The Meanings of Liberty

There is a story recounted by the African American filmmaker Melvin Van Peebles about his time trailing Malcolm X in Paris, in the week or so before his Oxford address. Peebles was interviewing Malcolm for a freelance publication when he nonchalantly asked him what the most significant development had been in 1964, what with the year coming to a close and with so much going on in American politics, including the election of Lyndon Johnson and the passage of the long-awaited Civil Rights Act. Peebles was surprised to hear Malcolm's response. The most notable event, Malcolm answered, was "the Chinese detonation of a nuclear bomb." In reflecting upon the statement, Peebles offered a simple explanation. "The cat," he said, "had a decolonized mind."[37] For Malcolm, China was becoming what Japan had once represented in the early part of the twentieth century: an independent and powerful nonwhite state capable of competing with the foremost Western powers.

Malcolm's view of liberty was very much tied to power in this way. To be free, one had to be capable of deterring attacks as well as inflicting harm upon one's enemies. Malcolm saw this understanding of liberty as one naturally claimed by Western societies. Its interpretation as threatening or even immoral he deemed a form of hypocrisy. When responding to a member of the audience's suggestion at Oxford that the "killing of missionaries" by the Congolese rebels in Stanleyville was an unacceptable form of extremism, Malcolm reminded his audience of the lengths Europeans and Americans went to protect themselves during the Second World War:

> I'd call it the type of extremism that was involved when America dropped the bomb on Hiroshima and killed 80,000 people, or over

80,000 people, both men, women, children, everything. It was an act of war. I'd call it the same kind of extremism that happened when England dropped bombs on German cities, and Germans dropped bombs on English cities.[38]

While this response offers a window into Malcolm' sense of justice, it is very much tied to his view of liberty. Peebles's folk interpretation of Malcolm is not off the mark, particularly when taken with Malcolm's overall anticolonial worldview. While the audience member's rhetorical question implicates Malcolm for welcoming the murder of some (whites) while abdicating responsibility for others (blacks), it fails to recognize that Malcolm placed the history of the people of the Congo—indeed all colonized peoples—in the same category, cases subsumed under "existential threats," as those assumed by the Allies facing Nazism. In the notes in his diary for his UK visit under the heading "Imagery," Malcolm offers his own pithy rhetorical question that reflects his critique of the chief deficiency of Western liberty: "white life worth more than black life?"[39]

In a sense Malcolm was railing against a view prevalent then, and perhaps no less now, that African people either lacked, or stood outside, a coherent sense of liberty. Popular histories of the American founding to this day traffic in this sort of analysis and, while they may not intend to do so, serve as a kind of defense for colonialism or, worse, slavery:

> Liberty, independence, and virtue were dear to the people of all four British-American cultures [Puritans, Quakers, Scots-Irish, Cavaliers] however their definitions varied.... But what of the last great colonial culture, that numbered no less than 20 percent of the non-Indian population of North America? We cannot know what liberty meant to them because almost all those West Africans were enslaved.[40]

In this interpretation, liberty is only valued by those who have it (or as Malcolm might suggest, those whose interpretation is dominant).

Malcolm's task at Oxford, and in his new incarnation as both humanitarian and advocate for racial justice, was to demonstrate just how subjective the concept of liberty was. It belonged to the class of ideas by which Africans and other oppressed peoples were beginning to apply "their own yardsticks," as he had argued at the beginning of his talk. It was a point he hoped to drive home in Great Britain and France, as both societies were grappling with the end of their own postcolonial visions of liberty.

Malcolm's very presence in Britain and France was designed to underscore and capitalize on the newly constituted demographic nature of both societies. In Detroit, the day his home was firebombed, Malcolm gave what amounted to his last full public address. Just over a week later he would be assassinated. His view of liberty and its revolutionary underpinnings, particularly for Europe, was among his most prescient points made that evening:

> Tonight one of the things that has to be stressed, which has not only the United States very much worried but also has France, Great Britain and most of the powers who formerly were known as colonial powers worried, and that is the African revolution. They are more concerned with the revolution that is taking place on the African continent than they are with the revolution in Asia and in Latin America. And this is because there are so many people of African ancestry within the domestic confines or jurisdictions of these various governments.... There is an increasing number of dark-skinned people in England and also in France.[41]

Malcolm saw very early on the complicated relationship between liberty for colonial peoples and its perceived diminution for Europeans at home. "Just advocating a coalition of African, Afro-Americans, Arabs, and Asians who live within the structure automatically has upset France, which is supposed to be one of the most liberal countries on earth," he said in Detroit, "and it has made them expose their hand. England is the same way."[42]

Where Malcolm had once seen liberty as tied to a separate nation for African Americans within the confines of the contiguous United States, he was now seeing it as connected to the emergence of a justly won freedom within America—and for formerly colonized peoples, within their own native countries. More germane to Malcolm's Oxford vision, however, he also saw the value and potential for Africans and Asians to emerge as equals within the predominantly white states in Europe where many had found themselves. Malcolm's visit to Smethwick was premised upon this evolved sense of liberty. With a minority immigrant population more Asian than African (Smethwick's immigrant population in 1964 was 54 percent Indian, 37 percent West Indian, and 9 percent Pakistani), Malcolm was hoping to forge political ties that went beyond a "purely black" agenda.[43] When Britain's prime minister, David Cameron, suggested in an otherwise strongly worded anti-immigrant speech in early 2011 that "We have failed to provide a vision of society to which they feel they [immigrants] want to belong," he was paying rhetorical homage to the dilemma Malcolm identified for England nearly fifty years earlier.[44]

"Black" Britain and Anglo-American Diplomacy

Since the *Empire Windrush*, carrying some five hundred West Indian immigrants docked in Tilbury, the principal port of London, in 1948, the issue of immigration and racial "cohesion" has only grown in Great Britain.[45] Within the space of just over ten years, black Londoners would experience a full-scale race riot and what the historian Stephen Tuck has described as Britain's "first lynching"—the stabbing death of the Antiguan immigrant Kelso Cochrane in 1959—at the hands of "Teddy boys"—a mob of young whites whose ostensible aim was, in part, to "Keep England White."[46] By 1968, Enoch Powell had made his famous "Rivers of Blood" speech, and it seemed as if the transference of American racial strife to the UK had arrived in full measure. Indeed, it seems as though Powell's address to the annual meeting of the West Midlands Area Conservative Political Center in Birmingham had been honed from his more recent experience in the United States, where in 1967 he and his wife Pamela witnessed what he described as "that tragic and intractable phenomenon which we watch with horror on the other side of the Atlantic."[47] The Newark riots of that summer, among other things, had made an impression on the Powells.

Malcolm's British tour—London, Oxford, Manchester, Sheffield, and Smethwick—thus presented a disconcerting connection to America's racial travails. And while the Oxford address displayed Malcolm's humanistic magnanimity, it did not erase the British Foreign Office's concerns for the price of "liberty" in either nation. Even after Malcolm's assassination, the simple matter of offering congratulatory remarks to President Johnson for his handling of America's racial turmoil was fraught with the potential for self-inflicted wounds. In a confidential memorandum, Prime Minister Harold Wilson sought out advice from his cabinet on the matter:

> The Prime Minister's Private Secretary has asked for advice whether the Prime Minister should send a message to the President congratulating him on his speech of 15 March [1965] to the Congress on integration in Selma.... The question of race relations and of integration in the United States is considered by all Americans to be a matter of purely domestic concern. It is also one which causes them acute embarrassment as an example of their inability to put into practice the clear intentions of their Constitution.... It is doubtful therefore whether a congratulatory message from the Prime Minister would be appreciated by the President, no matter how anodyne; and it could be harmful.

In the end, the consideration "if it was the other way round: i.e. we [Great Britain] were in a difficult position on some domestic subject

and the Prime Minister received a message from the President of
the United States—it would not help" was offered too late to influence Wilson's decision. The message was sent, although it was kept
"private."[48] President Johnson's telegrammed response to Wilson
affirmed the global context of racial conflict while underscoring its
peculiarly American framework:

> Thanks very much for your generous message about my address
> to the Congress. You are certainly right when you say that this is
> only part of a world-wide problem, and while of course we must
> deal with it here as an American matter, I myself am struck by the
> degree to which our people recongize more and more that our
> progress on this is a matter of more than national importance.
>
> Lyndon B. Johnson[49]

Malcolm undoubtedly would have appreciated the British government's assessment of America's inability to confer basic democratic rights upon its African American citizens. And he clearly
would have seen the "embarrassment" felt by the US government
to be connected to Cold War symbolism rather than a failure to
meet the substantive needs of its people. Ironically, there is a different type of containment policy suggested in these Anglo-American
exchanges. The desire to render the black struggles in both the
United States and the UK as "domestic" matters is suffused with
the understanding that to broaden the meaning of the black movement in either country is to encourage greater internal and external
opposition. The effort to connect the racial politics of Britain and
the United States was only encouraged—as was the case with British
efforts to reach out to NAACP Executive Director Roy Wilkins—
when information attained could be employed in the protection of
national interests. As Paul Foot suggested at the time in his seminal
work *Immigration and Race in British Politics*, "In these political circumstances, internationalism is left to the clichés. The international
interest is acceptable only if does not affect the national interest."[50]

Liberty for Human Beings

In his two most significant speeches before Oxford—the "Message to the Grass Roots" and "The Ballot or the Bullet"—Malcolm never uttered the words "human beings." He extolled the virtue of human rights in his "Ballot" speech to be sure, making the case some eleven times that the *civil* rights struggle had to be converted to a *human* rights struggle. But the discrete term "human beings" was not employed, and it is worth considering why at Oxford Malcolm used it eight times. The temptation to presume that Islam alone compelled Malcolm not only to tap into the universalism of God, but also to ruminate upon the words of William Blake and Shakespeare, may be great, but it is not quite sufficient. Malcolm's conversion was indeed religious, but it was also political. For while Islam had confirmed the universality of the human condition, the black struggle in America and around the globe validated the specific attention to racial equality. Human beings had rights and those rights could be fought for without respect to race, but they could also be fought for, and indeed had to be fought for on occasion, *with* respect to race. For Malcolm at Oxford, the liberty of black people—as human beings—was at stake, and this helps explain why the Oxford address was so representative of the new ground Malcolm was breaking. Oxford was not a speech devoid of religious meaning, but the basis for liberty laid down by Malcolm that December night was not limited to ecclesiastical concerns. What was notable about the politics of the speech was that during his thirty minutes, Malcolm jettisoned the rigidity of Black Nationalism and the sophistry of postracialism.

"If we look upon ourselves as human beings, I doubt that anyone will deny that extremism in the defense of liberty, the liberty of any human being, is no vice," Malcolm argued early at Oxford. He closed in similar fashion, reasoning that "when one is moderate in the pursuit of justice for human beings, I say he's a sinner."[51] The transference of *black* to *human beings* or from *blacks* to *Congolese* elsewhere in the speech suggests Malcolm was seeking to appeal not only to the black diaspora as such at Oxford, but also whatever spirit of brotherhood he presumed remained in the West. This was more than an effort on his part to avoid being trapped as a "racialist." Malcolm's politics had evolved to see the potential for radical politics to be defined by an oppositional mindset rather than one's genetic coding. Malcolm's exposure to white Algerian revolutionaries while in Algeria as well as his recognition of the spiritual capacity latent in white society was part of his calculus. In his interview with the BBC broadcast directly before arriving in the UK, he had argued that education was a far better and quicker means of achieving racial justice than legislation. When asked about the prospects for gradual change in race relations, Malcolm doubted it but rejected the inevitability of violence. "There doesn't necessarily have to be an explosion," Malcolm argued, "if the proper type of education is brought about, to give the people the correct understanding of the causes of these conditions that exist, and to try to educate them away from this animosity and hostility." What about the level of violence Malcolm anticipated in 1964? Was he disappointed the explosion he *hoped* for didn't occur? "That's not the question," Malcolm corrected, but "has it been explosive as I would have *thought*? It wasn't as explosive as I would have thought."[52] The Malcolm who sat down for an interview with Alex Haley for *Playboy* in the summer of 1963 was not gone entirely, but he was far less apparent, as Malcolm was clearly crafting a new personal and political worldview.

Malcolm's focus on the black struggle as a human struggle was highlighted in an interview with CBS's Mike Wallace, early after his return from Mecca. It was Wallace, of course, who had broken the story of the "Black Muslims" in the 1959 CBS broadcast of "The Hate That Hate Produced." Over the years, Malcolm developed with Wallace what the famed journalist described in his memoir as a "mutual respect, even a kind of friendship." The exchange with a clearly travel-weary Malcolm had to have taken Wallace somewhat by surprise, as Malcolm proclaimed himself an adherent of

Orthodox Islam and no longer a follower of the Honorable Elijah
Muhammad:

> WALLACE: Then the white man is no longer the devil and evil?
>
> MALCOLM X: The Holy Koran teaches us to judge a man by his
> conscious behavior, his intentions. So I judge a man by his con-
> scious behavior, his deeds. I am not a racist. I do not subscribe
> to any of the tenets of racism.
>
> WALLACE: And so you feel that there are good whites and good
> blacks and bad whites and bad blacks?
>
> MALCOLM X: It's not a case of being good or bad blacks and
> whites. It's a case of being good or bad human beings.[53]

Perhaps Malcolm's most significant contribution to American race
relations was his refusal to see racial differences as purely incidental
to the human experience. At Oxford, Malcolm attempted to convey
the complexity of liberty's meaning as both a universal human right
and also one retained by specific kinds of human beings.

In a sense, the United States has been wrestling with this distinction since its founding. One hundred years to the day, before
Malcolm's pilgrimage to Mecca, Abraham Lincoln speculated upon
the two-tiered quality of liberty found in America. "The world has
never had a good definition of the word liberty," Lincoln noted,
"and the American people, just now, are much in want of one. We
all declare for liberty; but in using the same word, we do not all
mean the same thing."[54] For Southerners, liberty involved the right
to enslave others; for African Americans it involved the right to own
one's body and labor. Such polarized views of freedom strike at the
heart of America's volatile racial history. As Malcolm instructed
at Oxford in speaking of "extremism," "they [the colonized] don't
mean what you [the colonizers] do. And when you say [it], you don't
mean what they do."[55] To come to terms with liberty as a truly universal human right, one must also come to terms with the legitimacy
of methods employed to obtain and defend it. This is the beauty of

Malcolm's invocation of the American Revolution at Oxford. "Old Patrick Henry said, 'Liberty or death!' That's extreme, very extreme," Malcolm reminded his Oxford audience as he neared his conclusion.[56] In effect, Malcolm was arguing that violence cannot be made unjust by dint of the color of the hand wielding it. Malcolm's projection of this perspective was best articulated in his "Message to the Grass Roots," which, in focusing upon American foreign policy, would be reiterated by Martin Luther King Jr. a few years later:

> If violence is wrong in America, violence is wrong abroad. If it is wrong to be violent defending black women and black children and black babies and black men, then it is wrong for America to draft us and make us violent abroad in defense of her. And if it is right for America to draft us, and teach us how to be violent in defense of her, then it is right for you and me to do whatever is necessary to defend our own people right here in this country.[57]

For Malcolm, this paradox was what distinguished the "Negro" revolution (always said by Malcolm contemptuously) from other revolutions. By 1967, King was making an argument striking in its similarity, if not in its vehemence, to one long articulated by Malcolm:

> As I have walked among the desperate, rejected and angry young men I have told them that Molotov cocktails and rifles would not solve their problems. I have tried to offer them my deepest compassion while maintain my conviction that social change comes most meaningfully through nonviolent action. But they asked—and rightly so—what about Vietnam? They asked if our own nation wasn't using massive doses of violence to solve its problems, to bring about the changes it wanted. Their questions hit home and I knew I could never raise my voice against the violence of the oppressed in the ghettoes without having spoken first clearly to the greatest purveyor of violence in the world—my own government.[58]

To be sure, there are important distinctions to be ascertained in these views. For King, nonviolence was a nonnegotiable principle. For Malcolm, nonviolence was premised upon reciprocity—a form of equivalency in moral conduct. Bearing King's retention of nonviolence as an absolute good in mind, then, the proximity of his and Malcolm's views concerning America's one-dimensional (and racially privileged) sense of liberty is unmistakable. By the time of the Oxford debate, Malcolm had, by his own admission, moderated his views on race. What he hadn't moderated were his views on revolution and the right of oppressed peoples to resort to violence when all else had failed. Perhaps the least appreciated aspect of this point is that Malcolm's arguments at Oxford went beyond mere rhetorical musings. Malcolm understood that his own life was on the line in the struggle for racial justice and human dignity. When walking down the old staircase from his room at the Randolph Hotel in Oxford, or in strolling through town as bicycles hurried about him on either side, Malcolm understood that death could come for him at any moment, and from any hand. "He was very alert," Shirley Fletcher recalled, when reflecting on Malcolm's demeanor at her apartment. "He saw everything."[59]

Fletcher's observation illustrates the ways in which Malcolm's discussion of extremism at Oxford was personal. None of his counterparts—not Humphry Berkeley, Chris Davies of the Cambridge Union, nor the Earl of Longford—could truly grasp just how fraught with danger the motion "extremism in the defense of liberty" was for Malcolm. And while Malcolm's travels reduced the likelihood of his assassination, they certainly didn't eradicate it. When Fletcher asked Malcolm about his own personal safety, he told her he didn't expect to "die a natural death."[60] Malcolm's ability to perform well in such a pressurized debate at Oxford spoke to his unyielding commitment, and that of so many stalwarts of the civil rights era, to engage in actual, rather than hypothetical, life struggles for human freedom. When Malcolm told Jan Carew and a handful of supporters before his talk at the London School of Economics in February of 1965, "It would be better if we didn't leave together," he was not engaging in hyperbole. "I can be gunned down at any time," Carew recalled him saying.[61] When Malcolm once famously responded to a reporter's question concerning how Negro leaders have fought for civil rights, Malcolm argued they hadn't, that they really weren't willing to pay the full price for their liberty. "What price are you talking about, sir?" the reporter asked. As he had so often, index finger to temple, Malcolm responded firmly, without missing a beat. "The price of freedom is death."[62]

For Malcolm, extremism in the defense of liberty was a rational act. That black people had to generate explanations for its necessity was the truly "radical" conception. In this way, Malcolm saw the reality of American, and indeed global, race relations as part of a system premised upon absurdity, a kind of color-infused, surrealistic world that offered you the back of the hand if you described it for what it was. He was able to portray that absurdity at Oxford in no small measure because of his use of humor. He was also better positioned to deconstruct the ills of Western societies premised upon white supremacy, because he had been spiritually nourished on something more than an exclusively black worldview. Thus, by late 1964, Malcolm could see, however dimly, a possible path forward, beyond an inevitable racial apocalypse. His own moderation—his embrace of Orthodox Islam, his travels, indeed, his increased cosmopolitanism—enhanced his ability to deconstruct the invidious moderation of powerlessness for the sake of peace. Moderation in the pursuit of justice was indeed no virtue for Malcolm. Yet moderation as a byproduct of introspection, and indeed personal liberation, had the virtue of making one's arguments whole and replete with universal significance. At Oxford, Malcolm wielded moderation as a weapon.

Chapter 4

Moderation: "It is no part of the moderate to refuse to fight"

Malcolm's journey toward personal and collective enlightenment, by some measure, drew him into a narrative arc of moderation. Alex Haley's *Autobiography* has in some respects been partly responsible for rendering Malcolm's life a study in the teleology of tameness.[1] The organization of the American edition of the text bracketed Malcolm's story with a *New York Times* reporter's account of Malcolm's life in the introduction, while Haley's epilogue provided the last word. The effect was to make accessible that which seemed subversive or dangerous in Malcolm. The British edition of the *Autobiography*, which opens with Haley's introduction, had the greater advantage of authenticity in that it at least gave Malcolm the closing argument, so to speak.[2] The "packaging" of Malcolm—a type of consumer-driven appropriation of radicalism as Thomas Frank has described it—falls under the heading of "the conquest of cool."[3] Today one can purchase replica "Malcolm X sunglasses" online through *Esquire's* website. The magazine proudly offers the following to its readers:

> **The Icon: Malcolm X**
> The more radical of our civil-rights leaders, Malcolm X was known for his unwavering convictions. His dress was similarly steadfast: He almost always wore a suit and a smart topcoat. But you couldn't imagine Malcolm X without his frames, which have become inextricable from the man himself.[4]

The glasses are available, at last check, for $980. The media's framing of Malcolm X, it seems, has evolved, quite literally. Reading Malcolm's political development through the prism of contemporary understandings of his "radical" connection to the civil rights movement, as the ad suggests, may indeed help "sell" Malcolm, but it hardly comprehends him. More to the point, the self-willed moderation of Malcolm X, particularly understood in the context of his speech at Oxford, was more about expanding the horizons of radicalism than it was about commodifying its legitimacy. As Humphry Berkeley noted, without irony, during the open forum after the Oxford debate, "It is no part of the moderate to refuse to fight."[5]

Of course, envisioning Malcolm X as a moderate is a difficult intellectual exercise. One can forgive the *Economist* for failing to recall that Malcolm's image had, in fact, been imprinted upon an American-issued postage stamp in 1999.[6] "Whereas [Martin Luther] King appeared on an American stamp and has a national holiday in his honour, Malcolm appeared on an Iranian stamp and has been lauded by al-Qaeda," the magazine erroneously reported in its review of Manning Marable's biography of Malcolm.[7] Whether Malcolm would have been honored to have his memory commemorated in either manner is an entirely different question. His paramount objective in seeking redress for the crimes against African Americans, while combating racial oppression around the world, compelled him to work at seeming cross-purposes. He had to at once address his distorted image, as exemplified by the early statements of his Oxford talk, and in addition, demonstrate a righteous sense of indignation—indeed militancy—which he believed necessary to get the United States and other nations to act decisively on the race question in America. Thus, while Malcolm took up the oratorical cudgel at Oxford, proving "moderation in the pursuit of justice" was no virtue, he also understood that the case could only be made by someone who had the ear of people far less committed than he.

Malcolm's row with Humphry Berkeley at Oxford thus illuminated the tightrope he had to walk. Berkeley's speech preceded

Malcolm's and was substantively and stylistically off-putting to him personally. Describing Malcolm as "an apostle of racial absolutism," Berkeley launched into his verbal assault upon Malcolm's name. In a barb somewhat misremembered by Tariq Ali, Berkeley lampooned Malcolm as a man "whose pseudonym has been plagiarized from the works of Kafka."[8] It was a witty line, to be certain, but it drew nervous laughter and muffled groans from an audience otherwise well disposed to Berkeley's wry humor. Thus, Malcolm, pitched by Berkeley as the "Other," was compelled to address an audience that saw him presented through the lenses not only of fear, but also ridicule.

Berkeley's more substantive charge was that the type of violence *he* advocated—Britain's "opposition to Hitler in the 1930s and 1940s," for example—was in fact, moderate. Describing Hitler as the quintessential extremist, Berkeley reasoned that "It is no part of the moderate to refuse to fight."[9] Whether this right to fight was to be accorded to blacks in the United States or in Africa was another matter, one Malcolm wished to explore in the debate. In some ways, Berkeley was an ideal combatant for Malcolm. As a Conservative Member of Parliament, Berkeley stood left of center of his party, drawing knowing laughter from the Oxford audience when he began a sentence with the declaration, "Speaking as a Conservative."[10] Berkeley, was in fact, opposed to racial apartheid in South Africa and racial segregation in the United States. He professed astonishment that his friend, Eric Abrahams, had joined in with Malcolm and MacDiarmid in supporting a motion emanating from Barry Goldwater. In effect, Berkeley was a conventional liberal, perhaps Malcolm's most often critiqued political type. And indeed, as has been discussed, "that type" became the focus of Malcolm's rhetorical strategy in countering Berkeley. But Malcolm also had to establish his own basic humanity and reasonableness along the way.

Malcolm presented his personal moderation throughout the debate through humor and identification with liberal orthodoxy. He jokes about meeting with conservatives up close at Oxford. He flirts with his insouciance with a young Oxford coed. He pricks at the audience's "racialism" for failing to agree with him on the right to resort to revolution when denied one's liberty. He scolds American lawmakers for failing to implement *Brown v. Board of Education*. He embraces Patrick Henry with winking irony. And he enlists Shakespeare in his defense of taking up arms "against a sea of troubles." Malcolm's arguments at Oxford, when examined carefully, are hardly unconventional. As he implied in associating himself with the revolutionary patriot, Henry, they are rather American. They are, in fact, quite liberal. "All the Arabs refer to me as 'Azieemi,' Muslim for American," Malcolm had written in his travel diary while in Kuwait on September 24, 1964.[11] Forty days later at Oxford, he presented arguments deeply rooted in American political thought. Malcolm— "the American"—had come to illuminate the nightmare, even as he could scarcely separate himself from the language of its most cherished dreams.

Moderation in America and at Oxford

The US government had a clear interest in portraying Malcolm as an extremist. His trips abroad were seen as deeply antagonistic to American foreign policy concerns. Malcolm's linkage of American Cold War prerequisites with the civil rights struggle at home drew the scrutiny of both the State Department and the Justice Department. As M. S. Handler wrote in the *New York Times* in August of 1964, Malcolm "intended to add a new dimension to the civil rights struggle in the United States." The columnist, whose introduction presented a more moderate image of Malcolm in the Haley *Autobiography*, noted the foreign policy implications of Malcolm's broader critique of US race relations:

> The United States, officials here [in Washington] believe, would find itself in the same category as South Africa, Hungary and other countries whose domestic politics have become debating issues at the United Nations. The issue, critics say, would be of service to critics of the United States, Communists and non-Communist.[12]

While Malcolm was making efforts to distinguish himself from his previous image, his adversaries at home and abroad were vested in retaining it. The BBC hosts during the evening of the debate showed a similarly strong interest in doing so, as Malcolm's efforts to link American racial policies to those of South Africa were dismissed out of hand in postdebate analysis.[13]

There is strong evidence to suggest that Malcolm had long been desirous of reaching out to college students and institutions as a way of conveying the seriousness and rationalism of his perspectives on race. Newly discovered tapes from his 1961 visit to Brown University confirm this purpose, standing out from other speeches at the time for what Malcolm Burnley, who found the tapes, noted was its "relatively moderate tone."[14] It is unsurprising that future foreign policy luminary Richard Holbrooke would be responsible for organizing the Brown visit. It was Henry Kissinger, after all, who was charged with arranging Malcolm's visit to Harvard's International Seminar, while the then-president of Yale University's Political Union and future Democratic Party nominee for the presidency US Senator John F. Kerry invited Malcolm to campus just days after the Handler piece appeared in the *Times*. In retrospect, Malcolm's speaking itinerary in 1964 reads more like one belonging to a member of the Council on Foreign Relations than to a fanatical "Black Muslim" radical.[15]

As was the case with other universities, Oxford provided Malcolm with the opportunity to demonstrate his intellectual bona fides while unmasking the presumed moderation of American liberals. What liberalism had established, Malcolm argued, was an underlying and prevailing acceptance of black suffering as part of the nation's slow movement toward civil equality. Prefacing his argument with another allusion to his Islamic faith, Malcolm declared,

> [At] the same time that I believe in that religion, I have to point out I'm also an American Negro, and I live in a society whose

social system is based upon the castration of the Black man, whose political system is based upon the castration of the Black man, and whose economy is based upon the castration of the Black man. A society which in 1964, has more subtle, deceptive, deceitful methods to make the rest of the world think it's cleaning up its house, while at the same time the same things are happening to us in 1964 that happened in 1954, 1924, and in [1894].[16]

In years past, Malcolm's discussion of American racial politics would have been more definitively underscored by a scathing analysis of the inherently racist disposition of whites. At Oxford, Malcolm's emphasis is on strategies of political power and the need to decouple the "American Dream," as a standard trope, from the realities of white supremacy as practiced through public policy. American democracy's hypocrisy at home had to be understood in the context of its foreign policy abroad. It is interesting to note that Malcolm does not mention Kennedy at Oxford, although he alludes to his administration's domestic and foreign policies. He did make the link explicitly in London, just a few months later, where at the London School of Economics he argued that Kennedy's "new approach" to civil rights—a more "friendly face" backed by the power of "dollars"—amounted to nothing more than tokenism. "The whole world thinks that America's race problem is being solved, when actually the masses of Black people in America are still living in the ghettoes and the slums," he said. "They still are the victims of inferior housing; they are still the victims of a segregated school system, which gives them inferior education."[17] It is clear that while Malcolm had become more hopeful about the possibilities of blacks and whites working in concert to address the entrenched conditions of racial and economic oppression before his death, he remained deeply skeptical about America's ability to confront these challenges in any way devoid of crass self-interest.

Moderation in America

"If one absolutely had to foresee the future," the Frenchman Alexis de Tocqueville wrote of America in 1835, "I would say that, following the probable course of things, the abolition of slavery in the South will increase the repugnance for blacks felt by the white population."[18] No one cast greater light on that repugnance and its persistence in the twentieth century than Malcolm X. One hundred thirty years later, that emotion's legitimacy, however challenged in law, refused to subside of its own accord. Malcolm's recognition of the limits of legislative victories reflected his astute understanding of politics—that fear and the desire to maintain power were as much a part of the dynamics of electoral reason as any greater sense of the common good. In fact, the latter was in all likelihood predicated upon the former. This is why Malcolm was so stern in his rejection of moderation. Kennedy's liberalism may have been real relative to the racial worldview of men such as George Wallace—or Barry Goldwater for that matter—but its effect was to cloud the path toward systemic change. And that change had to be radical. Racial justice in the United States required extremism, and in making that case, Malcolm found himself at Oxford not so much defending Goldwater as attacking the kind of half measures that stalled real progress.

By late 1964, the United States had witnessed a progression of civil rights acts, from the all but toothless 1957 act to the slightly less anemic 1960 law; to the 1964 act, which has over time become the most sweeping legal basis for racial justice since Reconstruction. And yet, Malcolm argued at the time, the US government lacked the will to enforce this legislation, using the *Brown* decision as an object lesson. "If they can't enforce *this* law," he said at Oxford, referring to *Brown*, "they'll never enforce *those* laws."[19] The premise went beyond an attitudinal discomfort with whites; Malcolm's astute deconstruction of the Senate's seniority system at Oxford, his analysis of committee work in Congress, and his visceral understanding of the role of racist terror in American society were all presented in universalist terms. "I don't believe in any form of unjustified extremism," he argued, nearing his conclusion. "But I believe that when a man is exercising extremism, a human being is exercising extremism in defense of liberty for human beings, it's no vice. And when one is moderate in the pursuit of justice for human beings, I say he is a sinner."[20] This repetition of "human beings" was not accidental, as Malcolm corrected himself when making the case for a "man's" right to liberty to liberty for the broader human family. The repetition had the effect of defining the broader objective of justice, as did his earlier rhetorical shift at Oxford from "blacks" to "Congolese." At Oxford, Malcolm's circle of "we" was at its most encompassing expanse in his life.

Meanwhile, the results of the election of 1964 were producing their own shifts among moderates and extremists in American party politics. The Republican Party was already engaged in a strategic repositioning, investing resources and ideological capital in an effort to win southern states from Democrats.[21] President Eisenhower's 1956 victory in five states of the Old Confederacy was a wake-up call to Democrats and was no small part of Senator Kennedy's calculus in selecting Texas's Lyndon B. Johnson as his running mate in 1960.[22] By the election of 1964, the GOP was forced to reconsider this strategic turn, one that would later be called its "Southern Strategy," for winning the votes of the region's white population disaffected with the national push for civil rights for African Americans. The Goldwater defeat in some ways strengthened the idea that the investment in the South could pay dividends, as it was the one area of the country where Goldwater was not humiliated. As the *New York Times* reported after Goldwater's defeat, moderates such as "Gov. George Romney of Michigan appealed for unity and urged fellow leaders to avoid hasty action that might split the party."[23]

Romney's pleadings were echoed by what would prove to be some of the last vestiges of progressive Republican voices over the next fifty years. As noted earlier, by the 1980s, Goldwater himself would be viewed by President Reagan as overly moderate. In hindsight, the deeper meaning of the 1964 election proved to be found in the fine print of Johnson's victory, as the *Times* reported a very different perspective in the South, one quite at odds with the mainstream GOP conventional wisdom at the time:

> The dismay and anger of non-Southern Republicans contrasted with the elation of those in Alabama, Mississippi, Louisiana, Georgia and South Carolina. The conservative Mr. Goldwater not only carried those Deep Southern states but also helped to elect seven Republican Congressmen in them for the first time since the post– Civil War Reconstruction era.

It didn't take long for Northerners to learn that Johnson's enactment of the Civil Rights Act (and, a year later, the Voting Rights Act) would lead to a torrent of white backlash. As Rick Perlstein noted in his biography of Richard Nixon, the Southern Strategy's test run came as early as 1965. "The South was supposed to be becoming more like the rest of the country," he wrote. "The results were a harbinger. The rest of the country was becoming more like the South."[24]

By late 1965, the civil rights movement had grown more militant and "Negro unrest" in the nation's largest cities was at the fore of debate in national politics. Dr. Martin Luther King Jr. began his first serious strategic consideration of black living conditions in the North and by 1966 made a historic visit to Chicago. The movement was spreading into a field of relations much more familiar to Malcolm. The poverty, violence, and threat of insurrection in America's increasingly nonwhite cities fueled white fears and provoked little enlightenment from the nation's press. A black uprising in Philadelphia during August of 1964, for example, was described by the *New York Times* at length but with nary an explanation for its cause. The closest the *Times* came was when it cited a "Negro judge who went to North Philadelphia to help restore order," who declared that the rioting was simply "the unruly acts of unruly people."[25] The report summarily noted that Philadelphia's black population had grown to about 27 percent by 1964. Speaking again in the UK two months after Oxford, Malcolm attempted to put the rising number of what he often called "Negro rebellions" or "reactions to police brutality" in perspective. At the London School of Economics, he argued:

> This doesn't say [the destruction] is intelligent. But whoever heard of a sociological explosion that was done intelligently and politely? And this is what you're trying to make the Black man do. You're trying to drive him into a ghetto and make him the victim of every kind of unjust condition imaginable. Then when he explodes, you want him to explode politely! [*Laughter*] You want him to explode according to somebody's ground rules. Why you're dealing with the wrong man, and you're dealing with him at the wrong time in the wrong way.[26]

The British Foreign Office had been investigating the political ramifications and national interests involved in America's race riots for some time. By the summer of 1965, the Watts rebellion drew increased attention to the question of international politics as well as the familiar consideration of the role of black moderates in the United States. The abrupt turn in race's geographical impact, however, was carefully noted by the British Embassy in Washington:

> Republicans and Southern Democrats in the Congress are already saying that had rioting on the scale which has occurred in Los Angeles taken place in a southern state there would have been "lots of legislation." But there could hardly be such rioting in their state, they add, because the older and more responsible negroes would not permit it to take place. On this, they are probably right, but it is just from their states that so many of the rioters have fled to look, in vain, for education and jobs. Indeed a certain backlash in Congress is already perceptible.[27]

The Foreign Office also noted China's linkage of America's racial problems with Western colonialism's demise. Malcolm did not live to see the dispatch, but had he, he might have drawn considerable satisfaction from the British interpretation of the People's Republic's response:

> Chinese rejoice in Los Angeles riots which are used as proof of thesis that oppression inevitably breeds armed struggle.... Comment has hitherto stressed class role of negroes but People's Daily editorial of 19 August seeks to make emotional capital out of incident in Afro Asian countries using argument that United States which maltreats its own negroes cannot befriend Africans or other oppressed peoples. United States actions are shown everywhere as aggressive (Congo (L)) and subversive (Congo (B)) as constituting challenge to Africans and people of the world.[28]

This was a prime example of the "yardstick" Malcolm described at Oxford being employed by the "changing centers of power" in the world. In a basic sense, the correlation required plain logic rather than an ideological commitment to Marxism. Prime Minister Harold Macmillan had made a similar observation no more than two years before the Chinese weighed in on Watts. As America endured its experience with what the British government described as "the nearest thing to insurrection in the history of the United States," moderates on the right began to slowly vanish, while those on the left found themselves torn between the sanctity of pacifism and the imperatives of militancy. The center could not hold.

Moderation in Great Britain

In America, the history of what sociologists have sometimes referred to as "social distance" has been closely related to racial demography. Since the inception of slavery through the antebellum period, the history of racial oppression—in both law and in sentiment—has been linked to numbers and proximity. Georgia, South Carolina, and other states of the Deep South with large numbers of enslaved Africans were far more apt to impose harsh punishments upon acts that defied the color line. Racial hatred has long been linked to shared space, if not shared status. As the influx of people of Asian, African, and Caribbean descent grew in the United Kingdom over the years, so too did the level of white unease, animosity, and what Malcolm referred to as "racialism." After 1948, with the passage of the British Nationality Act, which granted citizenship status to people from the UK's former colonies, a slow, but steady tide of immigration became part of a demographic transformation of Britain in the second half of the twentieth century. The racial composition of Parliament over the past 120 years tells the story: of the forty one "ethnic" Members of Parliament in the history of the United Kingdom, dating since 1892, thirty seven have held office since 1987. Nearly two-thirds of this group—men with surnames such as Khan, Sharma, Patel, and Zahawi—have been elected since 2000. In 1950, there were no "non-white" MPs—a category different from the more limited term "ethnic"; by 2005, there were fifteen. Oxford University reflected these changing dynamics as well, as the institution became less white, less male, and less privileged during the postwar period. And the politics of the nation and the university were compelled to address these changes, to grapple with the rise of extremist sentiments against this new field of race relations, something that was altogether outside the modern experience of the Commonwealth.

Despite the suggestion by some that "Oxford became less attractive to junior members from the Commonwealth after the Second World War because decolonization entailed the development of universities in the newly independent states," the evidence points to a moderate, but noticeable, increase in the university's student population of color after the war.[29] As was the case with the UK at large, Oxford was compelled to define its place in a "post-imperial" world. In some respects, Oxford was slower to change than the nation as a whole, as it was "much older than the United Kingdom" and had enjoyed relatively little external scrutiny.[30] By the time Malcolm arrived at Oxford, the Franks Commission had already been put in place to begin an examination of the university's administrative structure and policies, as Oxford's well-earned reputation as an exclusive club for the privileged was called into question. While hardly a pure meritocracy, by the time of the 1964 debate, Oxford was, like the UK, a world in flux. Malcolm's closest male acquaintances at Oxford—his host, Eric Abrahams, and his enthusiastic seatmate at the debate, Tariq Ali—were young men with white girlfriends. Women, at that point, had been admitted to the Union and were becoming a real presence in the colleges. As the sociologist Joseph A. Soares notes in his study of the modernization of Oxford,

> Within twenty years of the war, Oxford's world of Latin letters and privileged leisure was dismantled. Wealthy gentleman-commoners were virtually driven out and replaced by hard-working scholarly meritocrats. Indeed, the conflict between old money and new talent broke out explicitly over the abolition of the commoner's entrance route to Oxford.[31]

The world of privileged leisure notwithstanding, Oxford nevertheless remains overwhelmingly white at just above 87 percent of its undergraduate population.[32] More difficult to measure are the feelings about the ethnic nature of change to the university community over the years. Indeed, even the best studies of the history of social change at Oxford, including Soares's, pay little attention to the racial or ethnic makeup of the institution. The class and gender components are more central to most explanations of the changing "face" of Oxford. They alone, however, do not go far enough, as the presence of students of color was (and undoubtedly remains) an affront to some Oxonian sensibilities. On the whole, strides toward moderation—to change the composition of Oxford, to make it more reflective of British society and changing world conditions more broadly, were part of a national undertaking, one which would produce its own backlash.

By the early 1960s, few in Britain were under the illusion that the nation's role had been anything but diminished. Malcolm's early emphasis on this point at Oxford—that "times are changing, and the center of power is changing"—was to in fact become the basis for official efforts to reorganize the entire apparatus of British diplomatic relations. Lord Plowden's confidential 1964 Report to Prime Minister Harold Macmillan spelled out in very clear terms why change was necessary. "The world in which the overseas Services now have to operate is no longer the world of 1943 or even a world which could be foreseen in 1943," the report began. "The international scene has greatly changed and Britain's position in the world has altered." Moreover, Plowden's committee argued, "There has been an undeniable change in the balance as well as in the nature of military power throughout the world," necessitating the need to employ what more contemporary scholars would call "soft power."[33] Much of this change was a result of decolonization. As Malcolm had presented at Oxford, the UK was coming to understand that "When you're in a position of power for a long time, you get used to using your yardstick, and you take it for granted that...everyone is still using the same yardstick."[34] Now, Plowden reasoned that

> We are no longer concerned with our relations with a few Great Powers. Since 1945, no fewer than fifty new independent States have come into being, many of them as a result of our own policies. Their emergence has placed an additional burden on both the Foreign and Commonwealth Services.... The spectacular growth in the number of independent countries has almost doubled the number of capitals where Britain is now represented.[35]

This acknowledged need to streamline the diplomatic structure of British foreign policy was accompanied by other measures to address the UK's changing relationship with the Commonwealth and its subjects. The Commonwealth Immigrants Act had reduced in-migration from Commonwealth countries to a poorly disguised racial parlor game. A second act would be passed in 1968 to address the presence of Asian refugees from East Africa—Indians in flight from Uganda and elsewhere seeking protection in Britain. Meanwhile, in that same year, a Race Relations Act was passed to outlaw discrimination in employment and in housing. These laws had the unintended effect of pushing moderates closer to the margins in British politics. As was true of the conservative backlash to the Civil Rights and Voting Rights acts in America, race would be at the heart of British conservatism's appeal to disaffected white voters.

"River of Blood": The Rise of Powellism

As immigration became more central to British politics in the 1960s, so too did conservative—and indeed, extreme—voices emerge in fierce opposition. The night of the Oxford debate, future prime minister Edward Heath, originally scheduled to participate, was a last-minute cancellation. A late arrival to Oxford from Parliament in London, he was unable to face Malcolm X in person, offering instead biting, unopposed commentary from the BBC's studio. As a Conservative, and no champion of minority rights to be sure, Heath found himself a few years later having to dismiss his cabinet member, Enoch Powell, for what would become the most controversial speech in modern British history. Warning in 1968 that "in 15 or 20 years' time the black man will have the whip hand over the white man," Powell's speech to a Conservative Association meeting in Birmingham tapped into a largely unspoken sentiment throughout Great Britain. The language, crafted by a man trained in the classics, was not short on crude racial appeals, with Powell describing, at one point, black children as "charming wide-grinning piccaninnies."[36] By 1969, Gallup was reporting Powell to be "the most popular man in Britain."[37]

Among the more notable assertions offered by Powell at the time was his proclamation that "nothing is more misleading than comparison between the Commonwealth immigrant in Britain and the American Negro."[38] Powell, not unlike the BBC's commentators during the Oxford debate, saw the dichotomization of the struggle for racial justice in this way as useful, insofar as the American racial case was seen as "historic" and unique to America's founding. Conversely, British racial circumstances were seen as new or pending. Powell's Romanesque foreshadowing of a Tiber River (read, Thames) overflowing with blood was that of a man seeking to stem the tide (or as Margaret Thatcher later put it, the "swamp") of undesirable peoples. Thomas Jefferson's nightmares by way of example were at the dawn of American Empire, not its dusk:

> I become daily more and more convinced that all the West India Islands will remain in the hands of the people of colour, and a total expulsion of the whites sooner or later take place. It is high time we should foresee the bloody scenes which our children certainly, and possibly ourselves (south of the Patowmac) have to wade through, and try to avert them.[39]

Powell's other, less scrutinized invocation of Rome was equally germane. As the West's latest empire confronted its own demise, Powell hearkened back to England's classical connection to the grandeur, and by extension, ultimate decay, of Rome. Despite differences between imperial and republican rule, his Roman fetish offered suitable protection against the charge of pure racism or fear-mongering. If people took the comments out of context, it was a problem of historical ignorance. Such was Goldwater's defense of the "extremism" line. *That was Cicero, not me.*

While Powell preferred to avoid direct comparisons between Anglo and American histories of racial conflict, there was no mistaking the equally real sense of threat capitalized on by both American Republicans and British Conservatives. That threat was linked to color—its growing presence, and its empowerment ("the black man will have the whip hand"). Powell's apologia, if not apology, was rendered in terms of his religious faith. In his book *No Easy Answers*, Powell engaged in a dialogue with the Anglican Bishop Trevor Huddleston. Their exchange on ethnic and racial identity is striking:

HUDDLESTON: .... what I still want to know from you, really, is why the presence of a coloured immigrant group is objectionable, when the presence of a non-colored immigrant group is not objectionable.

POWELL: On the contrary, I have often said that if we saw the prospect of five million Germans in this country at the end of the century, the risks of disruption and violence would probably be greater, and the antagonism aroused would be more severe. The reason why the whole debate in this country on immigration is related to coloured immigration is because there has been no net immigration of white Commonwealth citizens, and there could be no uncontrolled immigration of aliens....

HUDDLESTON: Yes, well, our history has been a history of immigration as well as a history of emigration; we have had a wave of immigrants far in excess of five million all over the period.

POWELL: When was this?

HUDDLESTON: Well through our history, we have Irish immigrants, Italian immigrants, over the long stretch of history. You were talking about foreseeing things.

POWELL: Possibly so, but is there any real analogy?

HUDDLESTON: There is a very real analogy. Why if this "alien wedge" that you spoke of recently in a speech....

POWELL: Actually I was using the words of a Lord of Appeal [the two continue their exchange when Powell responds to the idea of the Irish as immigrants]....I think you've failed to see the essential importance of numbers and time. That factor has been utterly different in these other cases, unless one goes back to the Scandinavian invasions in the tenth century.

HUDDLESTON: But they haven't in relation to the total population of this country. As I have said already, I would be perfectly happy if there might be ten million coloured people in this country at the end of this century, and I would thank God for it, because it would at least bring some fresh blood into a very tired old country.

POWELL: Well then you see, Bishop, we get back to a comparison of judgments as to the future; and because my judgment differs on the likelihoods and possibilities and dangers, I cannot feel (as I understand that you say I should) that I am acting against my Christian duty in drawing attention to what I think I see.[40]

What remains unexpressed is why Powell, in stating his opposition to the proposed Race Relations Act of 1968, necessarily concludes that this new, "colored" immigration, is fundamentally dangerous. By 1993, Winston Churchill's grandson (Winston Spencer Churchill) would help revive Powellism for a new day. "[Britain's Prime Minister] Mr. [John] Major seeks to reassure us with the old refrain, 'There'll always be an England,'" he said, expressing concerns over immigration. "He promises us that 50 years on from now, spinsters will still be cycling to Communion on Sunday mornings; more likely the muezzin will be calling Allah's faithful to the High (Main) Street mosque."[41] A quarter century after Powell's "Rivers of Blood" speech, there was a new specter haunting England—the increasing presence of Islam. The old nemesis of color had hardly died altogether. It had simply made room for another. While Powell's speech may have gotten himself removed from office, its underlying sentiment did not lose its appeal.[42]

Moderation in Islam

Nobody protested the arrival of Malcolm X at Oxford. Whatever anger or disappointment there was, it was not deemed newsworthy.

University, local, and national newspapers displayed varying degrees of alarm concerning his visit, but, in relative terms, Malcolm's broader anonymity in England served to tamp down more vehement forms of opposition. And, in 1964, there had not been a 9/11; there had not been a British 7/7. The rekindling of the Arab-Israeli wars was several years away. In examining many of the British Foreign Office's documents from the Kennedy-Johnson period, it is evident that decolonization was a preeminent concern among British officials for every reason under the sun *except* for considerations about its effects on global Islam. Indeed, proof of the Cold War's underlying connection to postimperial British politics could be seen throughout the debate, down to Humphry Berkeley's jibes at Nikita Khrushchev. Islam, on the contrary, was a very remote concern, if one at all. While perhaps not intimately familiar with the man or his ideas, it is clear that the British public was curious about Malcolm X. Nearly two and a half million people in the UK watched the debate that evening on BBC-1. The *Militant* estimated the figure at "at least ten million viewers" at the time.[43] The show *Gallery*, which carried the debate, began at 10:15 p.m. on a Thursday night. That 5 percent of the adult population of Britain stayed up for what would under ordinary circumstances be rather esoteric fare speaks to the larger question of Malcolm's possible reach beyond America.[44] What they saw was a man making a radical, but otherwise familiarly liberal, case for black freedom. And this connection made by Malcolm—between black liberation, human dignity, and Islam—did not confound. And this was for good reason.

One needn't subscribe to the view held by some historians that British common law owes its origins to Islam to appreciate the religion's historic contributions to Western thought and civilization.[45] This was not Malcolm's purpose at Oxford in any case. But what was pertinent to Malcolm's argument was his ability to argue his case without in any way contradicting his Muslim identity. This was not difficult, for in orthodox Islam Malcolm found sufficient cause to advocate revolutionary tactics against oppression while at the same time validating his broader humanity. He may not have used the term "moderate" to describe his worldview, but in a sense, he didn't have to, as he was arguing that racism and colonialism had turned the world upside down. The moderates were viewed as extremists and the extremists as moderates. As for Islam, Malcolm's brushes with revolutionary ideology and individuals were more likely to be linked to his effort to garner support from sympathetic communists and socialists—both of whom he maintained a genuine skepticism of, at least with respect to race—than from "Jihadists."[46] As the Turkish journalist Mustafa Akyol has written, Islamic theology has had an intellectual tradition that had long embraced "Thales, Socrates, Plato, Aristotle or Xenon" while finding common ground with Locke, Hume, Kant, Hegel, and others. The modernist school traced by Akyol serves to remind those less steeped in Islamic theology that Malcolm's Lockean "appeal to heaven" written about earlier in this book, or for that matter, his emphasis on dichotomies such as the "House" and "Field" Negro, make perfect sense in the context of Western understandings of dialectical struggle. "Hegel was his man," said Khalil Islam, formerly Thomas 15X, whose conviction in Malcolm's murder is now widely disputed.[47] Despite any formal training in theology or philosophy, Malcolm's preference for the German philosopher G. W. F. Hegel makes perfect sense—both as a Muslim and as a revolutionary. Malcolm's opposition to injustice was both political and moral. "When one is moderate in the pursuit of justice for human beings, I say he's a *sinner*," Malcolm had said at Oxford. It was a word carefully chosen, delivered in a near whisper.[48]

During the last months of his life, Malcolm was honing his message with respect to Islam. Gone were any strong declarations about the superiority—or even the implicit benefits of his faith as he saw it—in his public addresses. Malcolm was not particularly interested in religious conversion as much as he was interested in political transformation. This does not mean Malcolm had given up his faith by any means, but he rather saw it as a personal matter. He had said as much in Paris. ("Whoever a person wants to love that's their business—that's like their religion.") In his diary leading up to Oxford, Malcolm's shorthand references to Islam speak to his effort to moderate his public image—to connect himself to not just what Muslims call the umma, or community of believers in Islam, but to the umma that makes up all of humanity. The train of thought can be seen repeatedly:

1. Muslim-Islam-Allah (One God—Supreme Being)
2. All prophets: Abraham, Moses, Jesus, *Muhammad*
3. Prayer, Charity, Fasting (Ramadan), Pilgrimage
4 Hajj is April, *Omra*[49] in Sept

In another entry, Malcolm outlines more of the same, this time invoking race as his lead-in to his remarks on Islam:

1. Not a racist: am extremist (extremely against wrong)
2. Muslim-Islam-Allah (One God, Supreme Being)
3. Simple religion: unity—all prophets: Abraham, Moses, Jesus, Muhammad
4. Prayer, Charity, Fasting, *Pilgrimage* Hajj
    1. Judge not by color—but by deeds, intentions, conscious behavior
    2. American "white" means "boss"
        1. Brohood—but a realist
        2. America no society of Brohood
        3 Controlled by racists, segregationists[50]

For Malcolm, America is the de facto extremist, standing outside the ideals of human brotherhood. Islam is brought into the sphere of debate as a veritable mirror into just how racially driven American society is ("white means boss"). Despite his own clear-eyed recognition of the Muslim world's own challenges with racism, Malcolm wishes to underscore the moderate, universal quality of his faith—and, by extension, himself as an individual and public figure.

There is every reason to believe that had he lived, Malcolm would have found himself within the modernist tradition of Islam—a member of the Rationalist school. As some scholars have suggested, the tradition, emergent in the medieval period, "appears to anticipate many principles associated with Western law such as rationality, objectivity, principles of individual liberty and equality."[51] Some fifty years after Oxford, Tariq Ali put Malcolm's faith in contemporary perspective. "Malcolm would not be in support of any Islamist group," he said. "He would have opposed the conservative social and political views they hold. And he'd be opposed to terror groups such as al Qaeda. That was not his program." Ali saw Malcolm then, and now, through another prism. "Malcolm was a radical and revolutionary figure."[52]

"Brother Malcolm"

The final speaker of the debate, Lord Stonham, a last-minute substitute for Edward Heath, has been understandably lost in the already scant number of recollections about the Oxford Union debate of 1964. But his talk did produce one extraordinary exchange that helps illuminate the power of Malcolm X's insights into race—and white racial psychology, in general. Holding the floor for over fifteen minutes in opposition to the motion, Stonham threw a rhetorical arm around Malcolm, referring to him as "Brother Malcolm" on at least four occasions. Describing the motion on extremism as a choice between the "Golden Mean of justice or the Goldwater mean of injustice," Stonham rejected the policies of South Africa and the Ku Klux Klan as "forms of extremism which I oppose."[53] But then, he caught Malcolm's attention with an oft-made analogy. "[There's] an example which may make my point to Brother Malcolm," Stonham began. "The Ku Klux Klan. They are extremists...their methods are vicious, obscene, and deplorable.... It would be just as wrong to have a black Ku Klux Klan ... that would repeat the vicious extremes of white oppression."[54]

Malcolm's interruption was barely audible. But Stonham yielded the floor for a moment, and Malcolm pounced. "If the Black people in the South are the victims of the Ku Klux Klan any form of defense or any kind of unit they formed to defend themselves, you couldn't classify it as a 'Black Ku Klux Klan.'"[55] "I certainly could not," conceded Stonham. He then proceeded to argue that "moderation is not synonymous with cowardice," citing his ancestry of oppressed English Huguenots and his East End, London upbringing. "All were born in wedlock," he noted, "which must come as a disappointment to Christie Davies," he remarked, as it seems Davies had somehow during the talk referred to Stonham as a "bastard."[56] Undaunted, Stonham, a self-avowed socialist, lamented his position on the opposite side of Malcolm's during the debate. "I am not and could not be uncomfortable with Brother Malcolm," he said, "and only regret that apparently he is uncomfortable with me."[57]

"You misunderstand," began Malcolm. "Your statements are probably stemming from a guilt complex."[58] The line drew enormous laughter in the chamber. And then speaking through the laughter, Stonham began a defense that turned the laughter into something like a collective cringe. "I'm quite serious about this ... I've employed colored people for many, many years. Many years. And it isn't just one friend. I do not feel uncomfortable. I regret that Brother Malcolm does."[59] Stonham then went on to cite his support for a bill to renew the Alien Order and the Commonwealth Immigrants Act.

There was a type of mercilessness Malcolm reserved for white liberals. He viewed their moderation as more destructive ultimately than the obvious obstructionism of the far Right. But Malcolm could not have known much of Stonham. What he knew in this case was what he sensed—that Stonham's bond with "minority causes" was predicated upon an unconscious expectation of privilege. Support for the underdog was premised upon not being one, of being afforded the luxury to "hire blacks." What made Stonham comfortable around black people, the "many, many" whom he had hired over the years, was that they were part of his keep. It was an Anglofied version of "white means boss." Malcolm did not sense this quality in MacDiarmid, nor in Christie Davies, with whom he got along quite well in the postdebate session and subsequent conversations.[60] But somehow Humphry Berkeley and Lord Stonham triggered Malcolm's racialized sixth sense. At bottom, what Malcolm deplored most in the self-applauding liberalism of the type he witnessed at Oxford, and many times over at home in America, was its justification for white power. Reflecting on Malcolm's legacy not long after his visit to the London School of Economics just ten days before his assassination, the LSE's student newspaper described Malcolm as "an orator and political leader of genius" before explaining his clash with the conventional liberalism of his day:

> On the one hand there was what can be called the English Liberal reaction to Malcolm X. Into this category fall those Labour Liberal or Conservative party supporters who express passive sympathy with the Negro struggle in America. They fail to appreciate the significance of Malcolm X's admittedly extremist standpoint. Although he continually stressed that the reason for his rejection of white liberal support was that in the last instance those whites would still identify themselves with the existing power structure this failed to convince most of the English audience and also those foreigners who had adopted English values. They felt they could never sacrifice negotiation even while violence was being officially administered....Malcolm X insisted that he was not in favor of a separate state for Negroes (or Afro-Americans). It can only be hoped that his views will not be continually misreported in the public press.[61]

Like the *Esquire* glasses patterned after the real-life version, Malcolm X has spawned his share of imitators. His British "knock-off" was a man named Michael de Freitas, who became known as Michael X (and at other times Michael Abdul Malik) after spending some time with Malcolm in London, where he attended the speech at the LSE, and later in Smethwick.[62] Born in Trinidad, Malik was radicalized in the UK, where he underwent his own self-transformation, in large part, resulting from his contact and view of Malcolm. It was a transformation in which he was, according to the activist Stuart Hall, only "half-remade."[63] With no organization of consequence, Malik was in a sense more known for being known. A prolific focal point for press attention, he lacked the political or personal discipline of Malcolm, despite becoming a kind of phenomenon in 1960s Britain. In the end, he was charged with a violent crime in England and fled to Trinidad, where he was ultimately tried and hanged.[64]

In thinking of Malcolm X as an extremist or irresponsible racial theoretician, most of these analyses are more than likely conjuring up something more like the life and legacy of Michael X. "There have been people like myself and others, who've been influenced by Malcolm X," noted Tariq Ali, some fifty years after Oxford, "but nothing comparable has emerged in terms of organizations. I never trusted Michael X, for instance. . . . We have had a number of jokers and cheap mimicry since Malcolm."[65] Christie Davies and Ali agree on that front. "Michael X was not in the same league as Malcolm X," Davies said decades later. "Malcolm X had a good mind. Michael X was plain stupid."[66] Despite appeals to the British government from a variety of organizations, including the Council of Islamic Organisations and Societies, Trinidad elected to hang its native son, Michael X, in 1974. It was a horrible death, but not of comparative significance in any way to that of Malcolm's. In a sense, Michael X's life confirmed the caricature quality of the media's portrayal of Malcolm as a violent extremist or small-minded racialist. As the activist Darcus Howe noted, "Michael was reckless, careless, and I never knew what he believed. He was part of the confusion of his time."[67] At Oxford, Malcolm had served to clarify his time. And he did so in terms made accessible through the virtue of his own moderate qualities. As Humphry

Berkeley had said at the outset of his talk, "It is no part of the moderate to refuse to fight." Malcolm agreed.

By the denouement of Malcolm's speech, he had reached a heightened emotional state. His last minute was spent savoring each word, each line, as they dropped slowly from his mouth. The pauses, placed there in contrast to the rapid-fire staccato of words that preceded them, added a sense of melancholy to an otherwise fiery and at times humorous presentation. Malcolm was now about to say something not only important, but hopefully memorable. He dropped his head down to look at his notes, and then looking up at the crowd, so full that Shirley Fletcher would describe it many years later as "rammed to the rafters," he began to read from perhaps the most cherished lines in the English language.[68] They came from out of the mouth of Hamlet. And they helped Malcolm X tell the world that night just how far black people—and oppressed people more generally—had a right to go.

Chapter 5

Justice: "To take up arms against a sea of troubles"

"I read once, passingly, about a man named Shakespeare," Malcolm confided to the Oxford Union audience, which was now hanging on his every word.

> I only read about him passingly, but I remember one thing he wrote that kind of moved me. He put it in the mouth of Hamlet, I think it was who said: "To be or not to be"—he was in doubt about something. [*Laughter*] "Whether it was nobler in the mind of man to suffer the slings and arrows of outrageous fortune"—moderation—"or to take up arms against a sea of trouble and by opposing end them." And I go for that. If you take up arms, you'll end it. But if you sit around and wait for the one who's in power to make up his mind that he should end it, you'll be waiting a long time.[1]

With that, Malcolm had plunged into the great existential crisis of modernity—at least from the conceptual point of view of revolution. The "paralysis" of modern society invoked by so many political theorists was, for Malcolm, an intellectual luxury befitting someone outside the realm of actual oppression. By invoking *Hamlet* as a symbol for human action—the *vita activa*—Malcolm moved the discussion of racial justice to the broader plane of human exploitation. Discerning an answer embedded in the paradox of Hamlet's question, Malcolm concluded that to "end the sea of troubles," one must take up arms—to *act*. Albert Camus had argued something similar ten years earlier in his long essay *The Rebel* when he asked, "What is a rebel? A man who says no, but whose refusal does not imply a renunciation. He is also a man who says yes, from the moment he makes his first gesture of rebellion. A slave who has taken orders all his life," Camus reasoned, "suddenly decides that he cannot obey some new command."[2] For Malcolm, freedom involved a fight. For blacks in America and those oppressed more generally, the one inexcusable act was inaction. Justice in this world could not wait on Allah—nor Godot.

Malcolm X was by no means the first revolutionary—black or otherwise—to quote Shakespeare. Nelson Mandela and his comrades on Robben Island were deprived access to Shakespeare's works as a form of punishment by their guards, so beloved were the revolutionary themes and cadences found in the Bard's work.[3] But Malcolm's appropriation of Shakespeare involved a delicate balancing of racial pride with appeals to humanitarian impulses. It could not have been lost on Malcolm how those universal themes found in Shakespeare resonated on a personal level with his British audience. It takes a certain kind of temerity for a layman to quote Shakespeare before a British audience, let alone one at Oxford. For Malcolm X— the "Black Muslim come to Oxford"—doing so involved its share of risks. But the reward of placing himself in the context of English tradition and the text most familiar to those in his audience, second perhaps only to the King James Bible, was too great to pass up. Yet Malcolm's desire to communicate in England on English terms did not involve obsequiousness or self-deprecation. By noting that he encountered Shakespeare only "passingly"—a word used twice to describe his familiarity with his subject—Malcolm was acknowledging the significance and universality of Shakespeare to himself and those struggling for human dignity; but he was also indicating that his "passing" understanding of Shakespeare ("I think he put it on the mouth of Hamlet") was sufficient to make his point. Malcolm chose not to disclose to his Oxford audience that his "passing" encounter with Shakespeare was actually far from casual—and that it took place in the Norfolk Prison Colony in Massachusetts.[4]

For Malcolm, Shakespeare as representative figure of Western civilization is worth having on your side, but by no means does his work reflect the totality of cultural achievement. Malcolm sought to put white Western privilege—indeed, all that Oxford had come to represent—in its proper place, all the while without dismissing or relinquishing the very best reflections of Western society. This was *post–Black Nationalism* and *anti-postblackness* all at once, in just a handful of lines.

One of the consequences of both his critics and admirers having focused so much on his means for achieving justice over the years has been the obscuring of precisely what Malcolm's ends were. He alludes to these in broad terms at Oxford, and he laid claim to them tenaciously in the last months of his life. It is a picture of a just society, one no longer defined by racial hierarchy (and it is racial *hierarchy* more than simple racial *categories* that Malcolm finds most appalling). His last lines at Oxford take up this meta-theme of power:

> And in my opinion the young generation of whites, Blacks, browns, whatever else there is—you're living at a time of extremism, a time of revolution, a time when there's got to be a change. People in power have misused it, and now there has to be a change and a better world has to be built, and the only way it's going to be built is with extreme methods. And I for one will join in with anyone, I don't care what color you are, as long as you want to change this miserable condition on this earth. Thank you.[5]

And then came the thunderous applause, with many in the audience standing. For ninety seconds the chamber echoed with the cacophony of handclaps, caught on the BBC recording such that today it is heard as one long sheet of sound. Malcolm's open-ended premise of a world being righted by revolution placed him, in the last weeks and months of his life, in the pantheon of political thinkers—including Martin Luther King Jr.—who moved beyond racially based or local causes to get at the radical nature of modern inequality.

"I'm a Muslim," Malcolm told Simon Malley of *Jeune Afrique* shortly before his death, "but I know that it's not in the mosques that we will win: it's in the streets and the cities, side by side with those who, whites included, want to rid the country of the racism that is eating it away. I too, was a racist, but I learned and understood."[6]

Prior to his leaving the Nation of Islam, Malcolm had routinely expressed belief in the organization's doctrine of inevitable divine retribution against white society. His *Playboy* interview with Alex Haley in 1963 affirms this, even as he was moving more steadily toward political rather than theological solutions. Robert E. Terrill is correct in pointing out that Malcolm "did not lay out a static set of precepts or formulae, and rarely articulated an explicit plan of action."[7] But on the subject of justice, as applied to blacks on a global scale, Malcolm had moved to a more complicated analysis of how to empower people of African descent. In an interview at the Hotel Theresa in Harlem a month before his death, Malcolm met with Jack Barnes, chairman of the Young Socialist Alliance, and Barry Sheppard, a staff writer for the *Militant*. The interview would appear in the March–April issue of the *Young Socialist*, and it captured the thinking behind Malcolm's Oxford pledge to "join in with anyone, I don't care what color you are":

> YOUNG SOCIALIST: How do you define Black nationalism, with which you have been identified?
>
> MALCOLM X: I used to define Black nationalism as the idea that the Black man should control the economy of his community, the politics of his community and so forth. But when I was in Africa in Ghana, I was speaking with the Algerian ambassador who is extremely militant and is a revolutionary in the true sense of the word (and his credentials as such for having carried on a successful revolution against the oppression in his country). When I told him that my political, social, and economic philosophy was Black nationalism, he asked me very frankly: Well, where did that leave him? Because he was white. He was an African, but he was Algerian, and to all appearances,

he was a white man. And he said if I define my objective as the victory of Black nationalism, where does that leave him? Where does that leave revolutionaries in Morocco, Egypt, Iraq, Mauritania? So he showed me where I was alienating people who were true revolutionaries dedicated to overturning the system of exploitation that exists on this earth by any means necessary.... And if you notice, I haven't been using the expression for several months. But I would still be hard pressed to give a specific definition of the overall philosophy which I think is necessary for the liberation of the Black people in this country.[8]

Malcolm's path to a universal conception of justice has been outlined by biographers and historians alike. What has not been considered as arduously is where the content of Malcolm's views on justice—especially as expressed at Oxford—fall relative to both Western and Islamic theories of justice. On the whole, Malcolm's sense of justice may be better categorized as Augustinian than as foreign or extremist.

Malcolm and Oslo: "I face the world as it is"

Writing in his travel notebook in preparation for an upcoming speech at Dartmouth College in January of 1965, Malcolm X delineated the problems facing the American Negro moving into the new year. These included "Inferior schools, teachers, books"; "Unemployment of [African Americans] is twice that of whites"; "Our infant mortality is double that of whites." And he scribbled out an intriguing observation on the state of the American economy: "Automation eliminating jobs in industries where [African Americans] are showing employment gains." These observations served as evidence that the United States was in need of a radical solution, one that would fundamentally alter its basic characteristics. As Louis A. De Caro Jr. has noted about the Dartmouth visit, Malcolm was espousing a position that remains a cornerstone of American realist doctrine even today—one simpatico with Islamic teaching:

In an interview at Dartmouth's radio station, Malcolm was asked if the use of force against injustice could be avoided and perhaps replaced by a "more peaceful weapon." Malcolm undoubtedly recognized that the student interviewer's sincere inquiry reflected the popular nonviolent philosophy of the day. He calmly reasoned in response: "If a peaceful weapon could be used to correct the situation I'd be as much for it as anybody else. But I'm a realist, and I've watched this 'peaceful approach.' "[9]

Malcolm's personal rejection of pacifism sounds remarkably similar to the most recent and significant word on the subject by an American—in this instance, President Barack Obama. Speaking in Oslo, Norway, in accepting his Nobel Peace Prize some forty five years after the Oxford debate, President Obama enunciated his own rejection of pacifism:

> As someone who stands here as a direct consequence of Dr. King's life work, I am living testimony to the moral force of non-violence. I know there's nothing weak—nothing passive—nothing naïve— in the creed and lives of Gandhi and King. But as a head of state sworn to protect and defend my nation, I cannot be guided by their examples alone. I face the world as it is, and cannot stand idle in the face of threats to the American people. For make no mistake: Evil does exist in the world. A non-violent movement could not have halted Hitler's armies. Negotiations cannot convince al Qaeda's leaders to lay down their arms. To say that force may sometimes be necessary is not a call to cynicism—it is recognition of history; the imperfections of man and the limits of reason.[10]

If "racialist" is exchanged for "al Qaeda," we have the same sentiment expressed by Malcolm at Oxford. ("The racialist never understands the nonviolent language.") The difference involves Malcolm's rejection of what Max Weber referred to as "the monopoly on violence" held by the state. Malcolm's ethics must allow for revolutionary justice to flow from the people up. It is what makes him a radical. It is what makes him *liberal.*

Malcolm's sense of justice involved the notion of equality. Restoration to one's prior condition, commensurate with basic notions of fairness, had to be the objective. The logistical focus on "how" (violence) to realize it, or "who" (now to include white allies) may participate in the restitution of justice, became secondary matters near the end of Malcolm's life. Speaking in the aftermath of Cassius Clay's victory over Sonny Liston in Miami in early 1964, Malcolm was interviewed by a member of the black press. When asked to clarify his relationship with the Nation of Islam in light of his ninety-day suspension, Malcolm was somewhat circumspect. But when asked, rather innocuously, whether he felt "we're making progress in this country" in American race relations, Malcolm gave the type of graphic illustration of justice only he could give:

> No, no, no, no. I will never say that progress is being made. If you stick a knife in my back nine inches and pull it out six inches, there's no progress. If you pull it all the way out, that's not progress. The progress is healing the wound that the blow made. They haven't even begun to pull the knife out, much less heal the wound. They won't even admit the knife is there.[11]

Malcolm's Road to Justice

When Augustine of Hippo justified war over fifteen hundred years ago, he made clear that a "legitimate authority" had to be its author. Over time, Augustine's fundamental precepts evolved into a more broadly articulated vision for the acceptable use of force by Christian actors. Those principles still undergird much of Western and international law. The critical component of restoration—of making whole the state or community upon which violence is inflicted—becomes in Malcolm's illustration the proverbial knife wound that must be allowed to heal. What Malcolm's theology—and more accurately, his politics—calls for is an appreciation for the fact that power cannot confer legitimacy upon violence; nor can the powerless be denied the right to use force outside the bounds of what the powerful deem legitimate. And, most critically, their encounter with violence cannot be dismissed or deemed somehow imagined. ("They won't even admit the knife is there.")

Malcolm's long-standing sense of justice before his break with the NOI was derivative of Old Testament understandings of divine vengeance and the restoration of harmony through God's hand. Islam was seen as in lockstep with this "natural" inclination to balance the scales of justice through retributive acts. "There is nothing in our book, the Koran," Malcolm explained in his November 1963 "Message to the Grass Roots," "that teaches us to suffer peacefully." Following Malcolm's reasoning at this time, justice was as much an act as a state of human relations:

> Our religion teaches us to be intelligent. Be peaceful, be courteous, obey the law, respect everyone; but if someone puts his hand on you, send him to the cemetery. That's a good religion. In fact, that's that old-time religion. That's the one that Ma and Pa used to talk about: an eye for an eye, and a tooth for tooth, and a head for a head, and a life for a life. That's a good religion. And nobody resents that kind of religion being taught but a wolf, who intends to make you his meal.[12]

Weeks after his break with the NOI, and shortly before taking his hajj, Malcolm provided another, characteristically vivid illustration in his "The Ballot or the Bullet" speech. "Any time you demonstrate against segregation and a man has the audacity to put a police dog on you," he warned, "kill that dog, kill him, I'm telling you, kill that dog. I say it if they put me in jail tomorrow, kill—that—dog."[13]

As Mustafa Akyol points out, justice in Islam was defined at the outset as "protecting the weak against the strong." The Prophet Muhammad included a double-edged example of piety's superiority over presumed racial and tribal hierarchy when he said, "By God, an Abyssinian slave who obeys God is better than a Qurayshi chieftain who disobeys Him."[14] That message was very much alive in Malcolm's arguments at Oxford. Neither Englishmen, nor Belgians, nor Americans should be privileged in the right to affirm their self-dignity over others—be they African or otherwise. Of course, by the time he was at Oxford, Malcolm was in the process of seeking justice from what Augustine referred to as a legitimate authority—in this instance, the United Nations—on behalf of African Americans.

It is apparent that by mid-1964, Malcolm had become somewhat skeptical of Black Nationalism's ability to resolve the problems of African Americans, global as they were. "Can the Negro really become economically independent," he asked himself in his diary entry from May 11, "simply by controlling the retail stores in his community? Who would control the wholesale houses from which he would buy his goods?"[15] Malcolm understood that if African Americans were to get justice, they would have to "extend the sphere of conflict"—an age-old theory for gaining political power—by bringing the black struggle in the United States to the international arena.[16] The realm of international politics was fraught with its own perils and power dynamics, Malcolm learned, as he saw the global reach of American power through what he had referred to in Paris as "the power of dollarism," to the State's ability to reach him in Cairo, where, he suspected, he had been poisoned by the CIA.[17] Nevertheless, Malcolm believed there were no viable alternatives for institutional change to be brought about within the confines of American law. Short of his romantic hope that those in power would become "moralists," Malcolm pushed for a global audience to help resolve America's long-standing racial injustices.[18]

Even Malcolm's hajj, which has come to be seen as distinct from his political work, was a venue for delivering a " 'sermon' on American racism and its evils," he wrote in his diary while in Medina. "I could tell its impact upon them," he continued, because "from then on they were aware of the yardstick I was using to measure everything—for to me the earth's most explosive evil is racism, the inability of God's Creatures to live as One, especially in the West."[19]

Part of Malcolm's objective while in Oxford had to do with explaining not only the political and economic dimension of racial discrimination in America, but also its psychological dimension. The "yardstick" referenced in Malcolm's diary in Medina was the same one he described during the Oxford debate. The darker and newly independent peoples of the world could only employ it, however, once they had affirmed their own dignity and self-worth. To that end, Malcolm described in his diary why descriptively racial language had to be used to achieve "balance," if not harmony, in race relations:

> It takes some of the same poison to counteract (same as antidote) poison. Europeanism has been such a strong poison for centuries it now becomes essential to emphasize Africanism to counteract it and Arabism to counteract Zionism—socialism to counteract Capitalism, etc. Orientalism or Darkism to counterbalance whiteism.... Thus the present escalating World Struggle (Cold War).[20]

As Herman Melville had once taken the formerly infallible patina of whiteness in American literature and turned it into a thing of terror in *Moby Dick* ("It was the whiteness of the whale of all things that appalled me," says Ishmael), so too does Malcolm render whiteness a psychic contagion. What is different about Malcolm moving into the fall of 1964 is that "whiteness" no longer stands alone as the cause of global calamity. But striking its privileged status down, at least rhetorically, must be part of making the world anew.

One of the better contemporary reflections on Malcolm's political project and its movement away from Black Nationalism comes from the political theorists Michael Hardt and Antonio Negri. In

Commonwealth, Hardt and Negri reflect upon Malcolm's evolution as a thinker concerned with, but not simply defined by, racial injustice:

> The quest for freedom...implies such a revolutionary proposition when freedom is conceived not as emancipation but as liberation and thus the transformation of humanity beyond racial identity. It is interesting to note, in this regard, that Malcolm X and Huey Newton eventually question and move away from Black Nationalist positions they earlier championed when they recognize a conflict between the nationalist affirmation of identity and revolutionary projects.... Only a project of liberation that destroys not just blackness as an identity of subordination but blackness as such along with whiteness and all other racial identities make possible the creation of a new humanity.[21]

In a critical point of distinction between colorblindness, Hardt and Negri recognize that forms of identity must be the beginning point for all revolutionary endeavors. Revolutionary thought, in other words, should not shun identity politics but instead must work through it and learn from it.[22]

Shortly before Oxford, in early October of 1964, Malcolm gave an interview to a London reporter during a short layover during his travels to Africa. He covered Goldwater's prospects for election as well as his rejection of the need for a separate state within America. Toward the latter part of the interview he was presented with the type of leading question he most relished.

REPORTER: Would you agree you are on the lunatic fringe of the American Negro movement?

MALCOLM X: (smiling) Well I think this, that America's whole situation is a lunatic fringe. Anytime you have a country that refers to itself as "the free world" and a "democracy" and at the same time has 22 million of its citizens who aren't permitted citizenship, why that in itself reflects lunacy, a collective lunacy on the part of Uncle Sam. And you almost have to be insane to deal with an insane man or an insane situation.[23]

Part of the insanity of the American racial condition was that Malcolm had to perennially justify his fixation on race and racial identity, as if he was the author of its centrality in American life. While recognizing that a truly just world would not take heed to the superfluity of skin color, it was beyond clear to Malcolm that that day was well into the distant future. Perhaps conditions would be better for him personally in Europe or, better still, in Africa. But that would be seen by others, and more importantly by Malcolm himself, as a form of abandonment of the struggle. Even the dream of a "Back to Africa" movement was now only metaphorical in his eyes. And while his personal safety was better secured while abroad, Malcolm saw the prospects of a life in exile as untenable. "Moving my family out of America may be good for me personally," he wrote in his diary early in his travels, "but bad for me politically."[24] Indeed, fleeing America would damage Malcolm's credibility as a spokesman for African Americans. Worse, it would subject him to the charge of cowardice. Malcolm saw himself playing a unique role in the black freedom struggle, and he was willing to play that role out until its logical end. In this sense, Malcolm was a sojourner, taking his case for justice around the world, only to return to a home not quite fully his.

The Case for Justice at Oxford

"Well I believe that we should use any and all means necessary to take out people who pose a threat to us and our friends around the world." The author of this statement was not Malcolm X at Oxford, but rather presidential candidate and former Massachusetts governor Mitt Romney. Romney's response was in answer to a question posed to him at the final presidential debate of the 2012 campaign.

The subject was the use of predator drones—unmanned planes piloted remotely and used by the United States against suspected terrorists along the Afghanistan-Pakistan border. "I support that entirely and feel the president [Obama] was right to up the usage of that technology, and I believe we should continue to use it."[25] The moderator, Bob Schieffer asked no follow-up question and the subject was closed without controversy or argument. The targeted assassination of "Islamic militants"—and the casual acceptance of the attendant killing of perhaps thousands of civilians since the policy began, speaks to the vagaries of American justice Malcolm hoped to bring to light in his Oxford address.[26]

Speaking of the Western air campaign launched against the Congo rebels during the crisis of 1964, Malcolm's remarks are a stinging rebuke to the cavalier spirit with which the United States conducts war against its adversaries today. "This is extremism," Malcolm protested. "But it is never referred to as extremism because it is endorsed by the West, it's financed by America, it's made respectable by America, and that kind of extremism is never labeled as extremism."[27] When Malcolm declares that the killing of white civilians in Stanleyville can be justified as a necessary act of war, comparable to the even greater number of civilian murders caused by the use of the atomic bomb at Hiroshima, or British and German bombing raids against their respective cities during the Second World War, he receives a cascade of groans and shrieks from the audience.

Malcolm's understanding of justice was nearly literal in its adherence to natural law. Malcolm believed that the human reaction against violence was the unarguable right to counter it with force. Weeks before his death he delivered a response to a question at the Militant Labor Forum in New York, which has become almost iconic in its blunt simplicity:

> I'm the man you think you are. And if it doesn't take legislation to make you a man and get your rights recognized, don't even talk that legislative talk to me. No, if we're both human beings we'll do the

same thing. And if you want to know what I'll do, figure out what you'll do. I'll do the same thing—only more of it.[28]

Whereas Dr. King's appeal to white society was spiritual—a call to rise above one's fleshly instincts—Malcolm's was corporeal. One's body cannot betray what is just. Whites needn't grow in their sense of justice; they must simply accept its universality. Black bodies and white bodies are no different. They will defend, claw, fight, struggle, and strive without conscious instruction. If whites will search their own sensibilities, they will know black sensibilities. Of course, Malcolm understood this would be, and indeed, had historically been, a great source of fear for whites. Malcolm hoped to use that fear on the behalf of his people. An appeal to fear may not be the basis for an ennobling sermon, but it was a natural weapon against those who refused to act justly toward the oppressed. And Malcolm illustrated that willingness to wield fear as a weapon by employing examples when whites used it against themselves. "If you want to know what I'll do, figure out what you'll do."

Malcolm's use of the example of the dropping of the atomic bomb on Hiroshima at Oxford, like so much of his rhetoric, was built upon years of thought and analysis. As the scholar Vijay Prashad has shown, Malcolm's understanding of Africa and the black world's connection to Asia was profound.[29] Malcolm saw both China's and Japan's histories as relevant to the black freedom struggle; he also refused to accept the premise that somehow the deaths of 80,000 Japanese at Hiroshima could be considered just, while an African American or Congolese rebel's right to self-defense was a form of "extremism." When Malcolm told Melvin Van Peebles in 1964 that China's acquisition of the atomic bomb was the "most significant political development of 1964," it was a statement more tied to his respect for the bomb's potential in Asia as a deterrent to Western aggression than to admiration for its potential horrors as such.

Yuri Kochiyama, the Japanese American activist who would join the Organization of Afro-American Unity and be at Malcolm's side as he lay dying at the Audubon Ballroom on February 21, 1965, invited Malcolm to her apartment in June of 1964 for a special gathering. Yuri, who had become Malcolm's friend, was hosting a reception for members of the Hiroshima-Nagasaki World Peace Study Mission. She did not expect Malcolm to show up to greet the three writers who made up the delegation, all *Hibakushas*—survivors of the atomic bomb.

> When he knocked and we opened the door and saw him we were all so excited—we could hardly believe it. Our place was jampacked from the living room, kitchen, all the way back to the bedrooms, and in the hallway, with civil rights activists as well as the three writers and some other Japanese Hibakushas. The house was full of Harlem-recognized civil rights leaders; white civil rights activists, and some Japanese that we asked to be host and hostesses. He said he was quite amazed to see so many people there and said he would like to meet everyone. It was one-third black, one-third white, and well, not quite one-third Asian, but his warmth just amazed everyone, and it was really just overwhelming, and everyone was quite excited about him. The Hibakushas asked that the translators not interfere once Malcolm got started. He told the group a little bit about his prison life and that's where he did most of his studying.
>
> He described the course of Chinese history and Japanese history and offered the difference that China, like most all Asian countries, went through feudalism and foreign domination, but that Japan was the only Asian country that was not transgressed upon in order to be occupied. It went straight from feudalism to capitalism; thus Japan was intact and strong until she was defeated in World War II. I think people were quite surprised at all he said. And then he spoke of Vietnam.[30]

As Shirley Anderson Fletcher would be able to attest to years later, reflecting upon Malcolm's visit to her Oxford apartment months after this gathering in New York, "Malcolm certainly had a presence" in such intimate settings.[31] But politics and the question of justice was never far from his mind.

The US government had its own interest in Malcolm's worldviews—particularly those touching upon China. Less than a week after the Oxford debate, the FBI dispatched an internal memo to its director. "American Leader Hails China's Nuclear Test" was the heading of the report, a collection of Malcolm's statements made while in Ghana in early November of 1964. "Malcolm X, the American Negro leader now on a visit here," it began, "today hailed China's successful explosion of its first atom bomb as the 'greatest thing that ever happened in the 20th century to the black people.' " The dispatch continued:

> In an interview with NCNA [New China News Agency] here he said that China's nuclear test helped not only the cause of Afro-American but also that of all people of the world fighting against the imperialists. He praised the Chinese government's proposal for a world summit conference to discuss the complete prohibition and thorough destruction of nuclear weapons. It was indeed "a very good suggestion," he said. Referring to the present struggle of the American Negroes and the firm support given to this struggle by the Chinese people, he said that the U.S. imperialists would never loosen their grip on the 22 million colonized American Negroes before the people of Asia and Africa cast off the yoke of imperialism and became strong.[32]

The dispatch was declassified twenty years later.

Malcolm may not have had an overarching ideology, yet his pragmatism has been overstated in at least one regard. Malcolm's refusal to disentangle colonialism, racism, international affairs, politics, and history from each other reflected a sophisticated view of modern affairs. Malcolm saw a Negro church bombing in Alabama through the same lens as an air bombing raid in the Congo. It was, as he, and so many of his biographers came to believe, at the heart of why he came to be regarded as truly dangerous—a proto-"Black Messiah," as J. Edgar Hoover had anticipated, in his years as FBI director. "Malcolm X might have been such a 'messiah'; he is the martyr of the movement today," ran the Bureau's infamous 1968 memo.[33] It wasn't Malcolm's theology, but rather his present-world politics that provoked fear at home and abroad. Thinking about the dinner she had with Malcolm and a half-dozen or so students in 1964 in Oxford on the evening of the debate, Shirley Fletcher remembered something beyond politics that concerned Malcolm during their conversation. "He talked about his family also," Fletcher noted. "He had a lot of concern for his family. He knew he was not going to live very long."[34]

"Getting out the facts": Doing Justice to Malcolm

Oxford was the last, almost entirely unfiltered view the world has today of Malcolm X speaking. We can not only hear him, but we can see him. And we see and hear his audience at length as well—a multiracial and international venue at a time when Malcolm was just exposing himself to those types of forums on an international scale. And as evidenced by the BBC's interest in him—its exclusive coverage and contract with him those three days in Great Britain in early December of 1964—the world was beginning to take notice. Had he lived, he is likely to have gone on to the Netherlands to promote the cause of African liberation and the black freedom struggle in the United States. "We had talked about Holland," says Carlos Moore, who was with Malcolm in Paris, among his European stops. "It had the heaviest concentration of blacks outside of England. He was going to look into setting up an office there."[35] Compounding the difficulty in getting at what might have been beyond Oxford, Malcolm left no blueprints or plans. His diary is a wonderful example of reportage, but it is the work of a man on the run, with little time for reflection. There are no ruminations in his diary or other writings, where we see Malcolm revisiting arguments or evaluating his performance for future presentations. The Oxford moment for him was just that. Malcolm lived but a total of eighty days after the Oxford debate.

His assassination, made all the more disturbing today because of enduring controversies, resounds for another reason.[36] Malcolm's search for justice in this world continues to be fought in the hereafter, with new generations—blacks, whites, Africans, Muslims, Asians, straight and gay—all fighting over what Michael Eric Dyson called "the meaning of Malcolm." But there is much that is instructive to be found in how his life and death were recorded around the world in the days and weeks after his assassination. Carl T. Rowan, who worked as director of the United States Information Agency in 1964, saw Malcolm's death as potentially harmful to US interests. As the nation's first African American to obtain such high standing in the diplomatic and security community, Rowan was a staunch integrationist and a long-standing ideological nemesis of Malcolm's. The US government scrutinized Rowan's remarks about Malcolm's death, perhaps for their strategic value in assessing Malcolm's image around the world in the aftermath of his death. The Washington Capital New Service Wire comments of Rowan, declassified in 1983, convey his fears:

> Carl T. Rowan, head of the US information agency, said today that there have been "A host of African reactions" to the slaying of Malcolm X that have been based on "misinformation and misrepresentations of the issues involved." As one example, he cited the comment of the Daily Graphic, Accra, capital of Ghana. The paper said "The assassination of Malcolm X will go down in history books as the greatest blow the American integrationist movement has suffered since the shocking assassinations of (Medgar) Evers and John F. Kennedy." Rowan declared that "This will come as rather startling news to those Negro leaders who know that Malcolm X and his followers preached not integration, but black

supremacy and the separation of the Negro.... When first I heard of Malcolm X's death, I knew that there was real danger of it being grossly misconstrued in countries where there was a lack of information about what had actually taken place, what Malcolm X was, what he stood for, or what was being espoused by those Negroes with whom Malcolm X was in conflict. Thus I asked my colleagues in the agency to do an extra-zealous job of getting out the facts, of informing the world in order that we might minimize damaging reactions based on emotion, prejudice and misinformation.[37]

Rowan's sentiments were squarely in line with US Cold War imperatives. They captured US foreign policy interests better than the more comprehensive but more complicated analysis of where Malcolm stood intellectually in the last months of his life. There is nothing in the Oxford address, for example, to confirm Rowan's "black supremacist" view of Malcolm. The "image-making" of the West that Malcolm had so skillfully exposed throughout his Oxford talk was very much at hand with respect to his death. The United States ultimately had a vested interest in ignoring any change in Malcolm, change that would make his views more, rather than less, transferable on the international stage.

The British press's coverage of Malcolm's death was decidedly more mixed and nuanced. At times it was effusive. And the British government's internal dispatches convey a greater sense for Malcolm's evolution as a thinker and as a man over the last year of his life. Richard E. Webb, for example, who had followed Malcolm's rising influence within the American civil rights movement over the years for the UK, reported back to the British Foreign office after the assassination. Filing his report with great detail, he focused, interestingly enough, on Malcolm's transformation in the last year of his life:

> Since his last trip to Mecca, when he was given some instruction in the true Islamic faith, Malcolm's attitude had been changing. He has been saying privately that the Moslem religion is a far different thing than the religion taught by Elijah [Muhammad]. He

was saying that he thought Elijah was wrong, and what he was teaching was destructive.... He was on the way back from his extreme position to one where, given time to develop, he might well have become a constructive force in the civil rights struggle. His problem was that the more orthodox civil rights leaders could not believe this, or believe that he was changing, but from all the evidence at our disposal the change seemed genuine enough. Malcolm was never as anti-white privately as he was publicly. He got along well with most white people, and while he hated the system, he did not necessarily hate all whites. Nor was he anti-American as such.... His death at this time could thus be a loss and a setback to the hope of a peaceful solution to the civil rights struggle insofar as it affected religious and nationalist groups.[38]

Webb's thoughtful portrait could not be further away in its conclusions than Rowan's. Unfortunately, Webb's dispatch was filed for archival safekeeping by one J. L. N. O'Loughlin, whose cover note to the last official word on the life of Malcolm X by the British government would have made Chinua Achebe proud. "Most interesting," he wrote, "and a remarkable tribute to the confidence which Mr. Webb has been able to build over the years with the Negroes in New York."[39]

Perhaps the most favorable account from the British press came from the London School of Economics' student newspaper, the *Beaver*. Malcolm's February 1965 visit left quite an impression. "The fervent response of LSE's coloured students is summed up by one of them," the February 18 article read. "This is what we all believe— but we haven't been able to express it before."[40] That response was unsurprising, but after Malcolm's assassination, the paper's editorial was striking in its perceptiveness of Malcolm as a political thinker. Among other things, the editorial reflected upon the British Liberal and Conservative parties' failure to grasp the meaning and significance of Malcolm's "extremism" as a shrewd observation about white liberalism's unwillingness to extract its interests from the "white power structure's." It also drew attention to the very difficulties Malcolm spoke about with respect to his "distorted media image":

> There is no doubt Malcolm X was an orator and political leader of genius.... Since his expulsion from the Black Muslim movement he had obviously acquired a far more mature grasp of practical political organisation. He obviously interpreted world events to suit his ends but surely this is always the case. It is I feel because of his rapidly developing political ability that he became a menace to the black Muslims and the white power structure. For this reason, he was assassinated. Malcolm X insisted he was not in favor of a separate state for Negroes (or Afro-Americans). It can only be hoped that his views will not continually be misrepresented in the public press.[41]

The editorial was penned by the *Beaver's* editor, Tim Gopsill, and remains among the more balanced perspectives of Malcolm's life by any member of the white press in the period shortly after his death.

Two days after the LSE's student paper's story ran, Oxford University's *Isis* published a story on James Baldwin's visit to the Union. In it, Baldwin reflected at great length upon the racial climate in the United States and the meaning of Malcolm X's death. "Now from the public point of view, and even from another point of view not so public, Malcolm and I did not agree," Baldwin began. "He was a Black Moslem Leader and then he was a Black Nationalist, and I have been neither. Yet we knew some of the same things because we were produced by the same circumstances; we are in revolt in different ways against the same conditions; we knew the same streets, knew some of the people, had in common beneath our public differences the knowledge that we were menaced, and our families were menaced, by the same indefinite forces."[42] Baldwin, who had stood astride the worlds of Malcolm and Martin and had befriended both, then offered what amounted to a plea, one not far removed from Malcolm's final remarks at the Union two months prior to Baldwin's visit. "It would seem to me that, at whatever risk, one has got to try to establish a truthful dialogue, between, let us say, a man like Malcolm X and a man like Sir Winston Churchill, between a black man and a white man."[43] Baldwin was clearly more pensive weeks after the assassination. His initial response to a reporter for the London *Daily Mail* immediately after the shooting was less conciliatory if no less honest. "It is because of you, the North Europeans," he said, "the men who created the white supremacy, that this man is dead. You are not guilty, but you did it. He was not shot by two Negroes, he was shot by two Americans."[44]

The mainstream British press offered varying degrees of praise, contempt, or simple innuendo about Malcolm's life and death. He was described by the *Times* as a man who "wanted the limelight and got it"[45] and "a tremendously effective orator before a Negro audience."[46] The *Guardian* branded him in death as "Malcolm X, the apostle of violence," while summing up his background as "a former convict, an illicit whisky runner, and a university lecturer."[47] The *Times* editorial two days after his death ended with all the fervor a committed party-line should have. "He talked of a separate state for the Negroes, greater militancy, a new political party, and the eventual destruction of the whites." And then, perhaps the unkindest cut: "Like Mr. Goldwater, he represented a mood, not a policy."[48]

French coverage of the assassination was wide and somewhat diverse. *Le Monde* carried it on its first page, in language surprisingly devoid of opinion: "Le leader nationaliste Malcolm X est assassin par un commando de Noirs."[49] *Humanité's* coverage was more political—and suggestive: "Malcolm X Se Preparait a Denouncer La Collusion entre les 'black muslims' et certain milieu reactionnaires"[50] ["Malcolm X Was Prepared to Denounce the Collusion between the black muslims and certain reactionary forces"]. *Humanité* also captured Malcolm's transformation in ways that seemed to elude almost all mainstream press accounts of his death. "Following a trip to Africa," the paper noted, "and contacts with leaders of the integrationist movement, Malcolm X continued to evolve toward a more just conception of the antiracist struggle."[51] Unsurprisingly, *Le Figaro* invoked the term under debate at Oxford to describe Malcolm's death: "L'extremiste noir Malcolm X abattu a New York."

Carlos Moore and Lebert Bethune attempted to present a more complete picture of Malcolm to the French-speaking world in their April edition of *La Vie Africaine*:

> Africa became for Malcolm X a source of inspiration for the struggle in America.... His long and fruitful discussions with African leaders gave him the zeal that would guide him toward a broader view of the nature of the black struggle in the United States.... He waited impatiently for African peoples to support their black brothers oppressed in America. He intended to bring the question to the United Nations in order to internationalize it, thus overcoming the limits of a national framework, and moving toward a more comprehensive plan applying human rights.[52]

Moore and Bethune gave their own assessment of the already debated question of who, precisely, the real Malcolm X was. "The true Malcolm X was a completely different man than the one depicted by the popular white imagination in Europe and America," they wrote. "Malcolm X was above all a moralist. A moralist because he perceived that the African American condition had been and continued to be based on a false affirmation that white men were superior to all other men."

In his diary Malcolm can be seen attempting to set the record straight himself. In one of the rare expositions of his political thought found in either his travel notebooks or diary, Malcolm considers the role of race in his politics and the specific role whites are to have in the movement. While not definitive, the long-hand account appearing under the heading "Nationalists" offers a glimpse into what Malcolm wrestled with, and what the press failed to capture after his death.

Nationalists

[The] Racist position calls for too much time to defend this position and I find that most intelligent individuals are not truly racists but sometimes find the position advantageous. But my own experiences have taught me that taking this position demands too much time from the time needed to attend the problems confronting our people. Debates are consumed debating the racist position and this doesn't solve our problem nor does it open doors that are locked to us—and I consider myself an intelligent individual and if I didn't consider myself to be such, I wouldn't dare stand to represent anybody. I feel it is detrimental to our cause to reject whites from the benefits of nationalism or reject help from them that would safely help our cause.[53]

Even in private, Malcolm still struggled to find a term beyond nationalism to describe the type of politics that would bring about justice to African Americans. But he did not embrace "integration" as an objective unto itself either—nor would he. Justice had to be its own end and could not be substituted for with a slogan or process-driven politics.

We don't want to be integrationists, nor separatists. We want to be human beings. Integration is only a *method* used by some to reach the goal and separation is a method used by others to reach the same goal. Let us not confuse our methods with our objectives.... We must keep in mind that we aren't fighting *for* integration nor separation, but for recognition and respect as human beings. We are fighting for the right to live as free human beings. In fact, we are actually fighting for rights even greater than civil rights. We are fighting for human rights.[54]

It may be impossible to know if Malcolm ever wanted these or his other notes in his diary or travel notebooks to be made public. Given his sense of history and his clear appreciation for the growth of his public persona in 1964, it is fair to reason that he assumed that they might well become widely known. But Malcolm lacked the time to chronicle these perspectives systematically, and despite the *Guardian*'s error, he was no university lecturer, with stockpiles of notes or treatises waiting to be published. The term "public intellectual" has become a form of academic pablum in recent years. Malcolm may have best embodied the full meaning of the expression—from outside the academy.

Oxford and Memory

Tim Gopsill was twenty years old when he was the editor of the *Beaver* at the London School of Economics when Malcolm X spoke there in February of 1965. "I did meet him, but I have no memory of the talk at all," he told me.[55] Gopsill, now recently retired from serving as editor of *The Journalist* magazine, the in-house publication for Great Britain's National Union of Journalists, did recall something about Malcolm. "He was quite intimidating. It had something to do with his charisma. He had strength—just his presence," he noted before trailing off. Gopsill met Malcolm for about five minutes with a handful of students. The LSE was by his account a hotbed of political activity, an institution rather unlike Oxford.

> LSE had a high population of foreign students, with quite a percentage coming from what we would call today the Third World. I had friends from India, Africa, from all over the world. It was the number one place to study for people with political and economic interests.... There was a huge movement against the Vietnam War then. This was the early stirrings of the 1968 Movement. It was no ivory tower—I don't think I did any academic work at all. I was doing journalism and politics.

Despite the deeply political nature of his student experience, Gopsill, like so many who encountered or learned about Malcolm X's visit to England in 1964, find themselves today grasping to recall his speeches there, or how they felt at the time. This is not true for all who met or heard Malcolm, as we will see in the next chapter; but it does reveal how Malcolm's persona and his historical legacy have rendered him less understood, for any number of reasons. Gopsill, born in Birmingham, England, did recall the racially enflamed election of 1964 and later worked in a campaign against Smethwick's Peter Griffiths, who won the Conservative seat that year. "I heard that slogan Griffiths used, 'If you want a nigger neighbor vote Labour,' and I said, all right, I want one, so I 'm going to go to work against you." Gopsill supported Andrew Faulds in his successful campaign against Griffith in 1966. I read to him his editorial in the *Beaver* from March of 1965 about Malcolm's death. "Did I write that?" he asked with what seemed to be both amazement and pride. "Those were great times."

"You're the first person I've met that knows much of anything about the Oxford debate with Malcolm X," Stephen Tuck told me.[56] Tuck is a university lecturer in history at Oxford University's Pembroke College. He has written extensively upon the American civil rights movement and has researched, lectured, and written about Malcolm's visit to the Oxford Union. "You can't find anybody around here that recalls the talk or knows much at all about it," he remarked when we first met. Tuck's astonishment is well placed, as it is difficult to find those at Oxford today who can place themselves back at the Union and recollect the moment when Malcolm X arrived in town. Sir David Butler, now emeritus professor in politics at Nuffield College at Oxford, could only recall "feeling somewhat afraid" about Malcolm's visit.[57] Bruce Kuklick, an American professor of history at the University of Pennsylvania and one of the leading scholars of American political thought, was a student at Oxford at the time of the December 1964 debate. He too, could recall nothing of Malcolm X's visit.[58]

The same can be said of Phillip Giddings, now at the University of Reading in England. He was a student at Oxford at the time, active in the Union, and equally unable to recall Malcolm's visit. "I must have been there," he reflected, noting his level of involvement in the Union.[59] Malcolm and the moment seem to have eluded a great many people's memories. Perhaps Malcolm was too controversial or imposing a figure to contemplate at the time, a man one would just as soon forget—all the more, perhaps, if you were white in the 1960s, with the world seemingly unraveling around you. There were other talks at Oxford—ones better remembered by these and other individuals from the time. But Malcolm at Oxford remains the lost jewel of the American civil rights movement in part because few of those who heard him in the debate hall that night can recall him. Those that could, and did, remain the sole voices from a world suspended in time. They were there and they remember—the hall packed and the lanky, horn-rimmed, serious-faced man walking toward his seat in the chamber. And they remember why Oxford was important— to them, and to history.

Chapter 6

Virtue: "Authentic revolutionary"

Over the course of my time researching Malcolm X at Oxford, much of my thinking was confined to the question of who precisely Malcolm X was at that particular moment of his life. And I was equally intrigued by how his politics were being shaped by the changing world around him. But, near the end, I began to seek out the question of Malcolm as a person, as much as I did Malcolm as a thinker. I slowly, but surely, turned the Oxford discussion of virtue toward the subject of Malcolm himself. What did Oxford reveal about Malcolm as a man? Could I identify something within him that spoke not only to his worldview or the times, but, more deeply, to his character? I sought it out in hindsight, going back to my discussions with those who remembered him in the days and weeks closest to his Oxford visit; to the places he visited—Paris, Oxford, London, and Smethwick. Was Malcolm X at Oxford Union—the man who had converted to Sunni Islam and rejected racial segregation and racial essentialism—the product of pragmatic politics alone? Could one even talk about "Malcolm X" in the singular, given his many seeming incarnations? And so I went back to the many conversations and places that made up my window into Malcolm.

I began with Tariq Ali and those who spent time with him in Oxford.

"*Really*? Is that right?" The familiar and richly toned voice on the phone had an air of genuine surprise. I called Ali at midday from outside the National Archives in Kew, England. He was incredulous to learn how difficult a task it was to find people who recalled the debate featuring Malcolm X. "Well, Oxford was a cocooned place then," he said. "The Oxford Union debates were for members only and you had to spend a lot of money to attend. It was not a public place. You could bring a guest, but it was for members. It was not cheap to go either. But that hall was packed that night," he said.[1] Those who attended were mesmerized according to Ali. "The people in the crowd at Oxford, the faces in that BBC footage, they were enthusiastic, they were faces full of hope," he told me. "And that is why they gave him a standing ovation." Ali recalls Malcolm seeking reassurance from him as he sat down. "I remember, he came back to his seat, he was sitting next to me, and he asked, 'Was that all right?' and I told him, 'Look at this place! Look at everyone!'"[2]

When the debate over extremism had ended, Malcolm had won himself many admirers, if not adherents. He "lost" the debate in the most conventional sense. The official notes of the meeting of December 3, 1964, tell only part of the story. "And when there appeared for the motion 137 votes and against the motion 228 votes the President [Eric Abrahams] declared the motion defeated by 91 votes and the house stood and adjourned at 11:55 p.m."[3] "Winning" the debate was an unlikely interest of Malcolm's. His "long, twilight struggle" was to be fought against racism and its effects and could not be won with words alone. But if moderation stood as a preeminent classical virtue, so too did courage—the one making all the other virtues possible. And at Oxford, as he had done in so many venues before, Malcolm displayed it unapologetically. Despite how agitated he was over Humphry Berkeley's barbs, he regained composure and was gracious to his Oxford hosts and fellow debaters.

Christie Davies, who spoke first that evening, recalls Malcolm as a different creature postdebate.

> What I most remember is the difference between the public man and the man whom I spent the rest of the evening with. He was much more conciliatory in private. If I could say the same thing in a different way—if he'd lived longer he would not have been a revolutionary. After the debate, he was much more relaxed and we talked. He told me, "You were very close to persuading me." I was

glad just to have had a chance to talk to him. My sense was that during the debate he was keeping up with what he had to be in public. He was coming to see things change.[4]

Davies, now a professor emeritus of sociology at the University of Reading in England, found Malcolm's warmth a harbinger of things to come. "He was the picture of a man in transition. A man who'd been radical because he'd been excluded," he told me. "He was in the process of change. I was surprised that we got on so well."[5] And yet so much of what has been recorded about Malcolm's private interactions with whites—be they students, policemen, journalists, or the many strangers he encountered in his travels—suggests that he was almost always likable, respectful, and, perhaps surprising to so many of his acquaintances, *human.* The man whites ran into ran counter to the caricature presented to them so often by the media. Malcolm's display of humor at Oxford, for example, was not "staged." It was a simple reflection of who he was. The necessary politics of extremism did not extend into the sphere of personal human interaction—what Paul Gilroy has called the politics of "conviviality."[6]

Ali and Davies remain among the very few living participants from the Oxford debate. Their memories of Malcolm, for the most part, fit the sparse written accounts of the event. But in getting to the larger question of Malcolm's virtue, a notable discrepancy arose in reviewing Malcolm's time at Oxford—particularly Eric Abrahams's account of Malcolm's time in his apartment. Abrahams's taped conversation, recorded in Jan Carew's book on Malcolm's travels in Europe, includes a vivid account of Malcolm regaling Oxford students into the wee hours of the morning over the course of his three evenings in Oxford.

> So every night he came to my apartment during the time he was there. And that was an experience!...And Malcolm would hold forth every night during the four nights and four days he was there....I was sharing this apartment with

Richard Fletcher—Richard is now with the American Development Bank—and we opened the doors between our two rooms,
and sort of turned the two rooms into a mini-mall.... Here was this
man talking about racial injustice, and well he didn't mince words.
If you looked at his thoughts, they were not violent thoughts, they
were reasoned thoughts. But his language was violent. I really mean
it, he didn't mince words! And seeing those white kids cheering
this man who was talking about white oppression was really something. I remember that very clearly.[7]

I asked Tariq Ali about these nights at Abrahams's flat. What did he
think of it? "It is pure fantasy," he told me. "That never happened."[8]

It was Ali, of course, who was the last person to speak with
Malcolm the evening of the debate. This remains undisputed. But
what Ali said next deepened the mystery of what Malcolm did over
the course of his three evenings in Oxford. "Malcolm stayed in
Oxford one night and I spoke with him about a quarter to midnight
before he went to his room at the Randolph. I was gated as well [as
Abrahams]. I lived very close to Eric in fact... it is just not true."[9] In
light of these contradictions, I had decided to contact Abrahams as
best I could, knowing he had grown ill in recent years. My initial for-
ays into his contact information were stopped cold, as a number of
news accounts began to appear of him in online searches: "Anthony
Abrahams, dead at 71. Former tourism minister hailed as a 'unique'
and 'brilliant' son of Jamaica."[10] The faces from the commemorative
photograph from the night of December 3, 1964, were slowly fad-
ing away. Abrahams's account had been so vivid, and Ali's rebuttal
so certain, that the days and nights around the Oxford debate were
becoming nearly impossible to reconstruct. But Abrahams had
mentioned he lived with Richard Fletcher at Oxford, so I hunted
him down.

I soon found Fletcher, now retired from the Inter-American
Development Bank, on a list of Trustees at a global investment
firm. Like so many others I've spoken to about the Oxford debate,

I asked him if he'd ever been asked by anyone over the years about Malcolm X. "No, you are the first one to call," he told me. "But I have to tell you, I have someone you should speak with—it is not me. I was in Bulgaria at the time." Somehow, as president of the West Indian Student Union, Fletcher found himself in Eastern Europe at the time of Malcolm's visit to Oxford. "But my wife was there and she attended the debate...she has quite a good memory of it," he said.[11] The next day, I spoke with Shirley Anderson Fletcher, who offered some clarifications.

Shirley Fletcher, it turns out, did attend the debate, and she did have dinner with Malcolm X at her and Richard's apartment the night of December 3. Fletcher, who has written on sexual orientation and been a consultant to a wide array of companies, began her education at Oxford.[12] "I studied at the Department of Education and was getting my diploma at Oxford. I was married to Richard Fletcher, who was studying law at Exeter College," she said. "I met Malcolm X when I was pregnant with our first daughter. Anthony [Abrahams] was my daughter's godfather. My first experience with day-to-day racism was in England," she told me. "I was from Jamaica."[13] Fletcher recounted to me that "after the debate ended [Abrahams] asked Malcolm, 'Would you like to come back to my flat?' and he said 'Yes.'" And what of the thirty–forty students Abrahams had mentioned—or the "four" nights of student activity with Malcolm back at the flat? "Well, there was only one night we had Malcolm X over. I should remember; I lived there. All the students were white who were there that night [December 3] aside from me and Anthony."[14]

Fletcher's account helps to piece together the timeline at Oxford. According to Manning Marable, the Oxford trip was planned as part of an overall UK tour, one that did not have Malcolm touching down in London until December 1.[15] If Malcolm had spent time in the Fletcher-Abrahams apartment over the course of the two days prior to the debate, it is hard to imagine Shirley Fletcher not recalling it. It is even more difficult to imagine her not recalling dozens of students present over those two or three days. So, in this sense,

Ali is correct—those rollicking nights with Malcolm, if they happened—they either failed to register with Shirley Fletcher or, somehow, Abrahams hosted them unbeknownst to her. "To be kind," Ali told me, "Eric had some minor heart attacks and health issues over the years, and maybe this affected his memory. That is the kindest way to put it."[16]

Abrahams and Ali were to become successive Oxford Union presidents of color—a true novelty at the Union. Both were charismatic and well known, and very political on campus. Abrahams had a "great personality," according to Fletcher. "Who didn't love Anthony? He was a bit of a rascal," she playfully recalled.[17] Unlike Ali, "Abrahams became more conservative over the years," according to Ali. Christie Davies saw both men as "elite radicals." Perhaps there was a bit of a rivalry, or as Shirley Fletcher recalls, "I think there was some tension between [Ali] and Anthony." Ali was not at the gathering at the Abrahams-Fletcher flat and therefore would have no memory of it. But his memory is apparently correct in that there were no other large student gatherings with Malcolm at Oxford while he was in town. The best guess is that Malcolm spent Tuesday and Wednesday (the first and second) preparing for the debate at his hotel, while getting about town during his spare time. What is most important is the impression Malcolm made on young activists of color in the UK at the time, well-heeled or no; his impression was felt long after the three nights in Oxford. I asked Ali to tell me about those final moments with Malcolm again, to help set the record straight, as best he could:

> I told Malcolm that night [December 3] that I was gated. I had to be back at midnight; it was a quarter to midnight. He said, "You're what? What is this, medieval times?" he laughed. That is when we talked and I told him I would see him again soon, and then he told me, "I don't think so." I remember my girlfriend was waiting for me when I returned home, and I told her the story, that he thought he'd be killed. She asked me, "Do you believe him?" I told her, "I just

don't know." I told some other people, some white kids, who sort of brushed it off, that he was exaggerating. When we heard later that he was killed, it was devastating. We went to the pub the night we heard that he was assassinated and just drowned our sorrows.[18]

"Malcolm was interrogating himself about everything"

There is a good deal of debate today—much of it heated—over whether or not Malcolm's evolving political thinking proves he lacked a strong moral or political compass. How could a man of such "reinvention" remain true to himself, or have a core, the argument goes. This reasoning guides a good deal of the criticism of Marable's biography and the implication that Marable presented Malcolm as a sort of intellectual chameleon.[19] The debate also underscores present considerations about his virtue. Carlos Moore, for one, resists the temptation to speak about Malcolm's future politics had he lived. "I cannot say what he'd have done had he lived," he told me.[20] Moore, still politically active and engaged, was in Brazil when I telephoned him. "It is hazardous; there are so many factors and complexities to be considered."[21] What Moore was certain of is that Malcolm was part of a line of revolutionary leaders lost before their time. "His killing was consistent with a pattern of that period when the most radical Nationalist leaders were eliminated unceremoniously."[22] Moore described as "pitiless" the killing of "Reuben Um Nyobe, Barthelemy Boganda, Felix Moumie, Patrice Lumumba, Steve Biko, and others. Thomas Sankara is sort of the last of the line in [1986]. Malcolm was part of that line."[23] Moore felt the assassination of Malcolm acutely; it was Moore who helped arrange his Paris visit and was responsible for his safety there.

Moore first saw Malcolm at a 1959 rally at the Armory in Harlem. By 1964, Moore was in Paris, "fresh from Cuba as an exile." Along with Ellen Wright, the widow of Richard Wright, and her daughter, Julia Herve, Moore set about the particulars of security for Malcolm.

The first thing, when he arrived, was to take a cab and go straight to Ellen Wright's place. Ellen fixed food for him, and there we laid out a security plan. We wanted to have a large number of people around him, and we wanted him secluded, so he'd be safe. We were going to have people armed to protect him. Malcolm disagreed. He said to get rid of any weapon.... He said: "Get me in the best hotel in town. That's exactly what I need." He didn't want anyone armed and he felt that he'd be in greater danger if he was secluded. He wanted to be exposed in public. "If something happens," he said, "let it be before the public."[24]

There Moore watched over Malcolm at night while he slept. "I took these cat naps while I guarded him," he said. "I was to take him the next day to *Presence Africaine* to be interviewed and to meet Alioune Diop and other Negritude thinkers."[25]

During their time together in Paris, Moore challenged Malcolm on Cuba's race question (figure 6.1). Moore had seen the promise of a nonracial Cuba dashed under "a racist white elite [that] was ruling Cuba under socialism." Moore gave Malcolm a piece he'd written on the subject—"Cuba: The Untold Story"—and he described

FIGURE 6.1   Malcolm X conferring with Carlos Moore in Paris, November 1964. (Robert Sine)

Malcolm sitting "in bed for some three hours reading it" in silence. And what of Malcolm's ideology in those last months—was he moving toward socialism? Moore was unequivocal. Describing Malcolm's relationship with the radical paper *The Militant*, Moore said, "Malcolm was tactically using *The Militant* to get his words out.... But he was neither a Trotskyite, a Stalinist, or a Leninist, or a Castroite. Until the end, Malcolm was very much his own man politically."[26] For Moore, it was entirely possible for Malcolm to be open to new perspectives—even radically new ones—without compromising who he was.

Like many in the movement at the time, Moore was "shocked" by the assassination. He had been planning with Malcolm to return to Paris in February of 1965. The Federation of African Students in France (FEANF) was to sponsor the second rally, "designed to launch the Paris branch of the OAAU."[27] And then there were to be other offices opened in Europe, wherever there was a sizable black population. Both Moore and the black novelist Chester Himes were challenging Malcolm on Islam and its own history with racism, according to Moore. "I saw he was deeply disturbed by what Chester was saying, which I fully agreed with, since I had lived in Egypt for a year after leaving Cuba," said Moore. "But Malcolm remained silent, just listening."[28] I asked Moore to describe the Malcolm who had given the Paris speech, just over a week before his visit to Oxford. "He was still a staunch Muslim," he said, "but not at all the same Malcolm I had heard in 1960. He was a passionate person, but even more eloquent and charismatic." And then Moore described the kind of introspection revealed in Malcolm's travel diaries and notebooks. "The Malcolm I met at that time," he said, "was interrogating himself about everything, including the Arab culture."[29]

In Paris today, that culture is being interrogated to be certain but in ways rather different then when Malcolm visited in 1964. The long-established policy regarding race in France has been one of denial. Arabs, Muslims, blacks—be they African or West Indian—all have been viewed through the realm of official government accounting as "French." Valerie Amiraux and Patrick Simon's study of immigration in France captures the policy's perspective best: "There are no minorities here."[30] Pap Ndiyae, one of the leading scholars in France on questions of race, noted that this practice of denial goes beyond the sphere of the French government. "At the university, for example, there aren't any professors that are specialized in the question of slavery. You can take a class about it, but there is no one person specialized in the subject."[31] Ndiaye has produced a modern classic on the subject of race in France—*La Condition Noire*—and helped found the political and intellectual basis for CRAN—the Representative Council of Black Associations in France—the umbrella organization for black groups in the country. Ndiaye sees France's aversion to broader racial questions as stemming from "classic republican reasons." But he adds, "It's [also] because of the classic Marxist perspective which states that inequality is based on class. Other forms of inequality, like racism, get swept under the rug or are seen as a smokescreen. The idea is that once the problem of class inequality is dealt with, then the problem of race will disappear."[32]

Ndiaye, whose mother is French and father Senegalese, is a professor in history at Sciences Po in Paris. When we met near his office for lunch, I asked him to help put Malcolm X's legacy in France in perspective. Ndiaye began with Malcolm's genuineness:

> We've had many imitations. He's talked about in hip-hop music, [where] he's well known. He's an iconic figure of postmodernity, like Che Guevara. There's this sort of romantic "hello" to these figures, but that doesn't mean we delve into who this figure really is. His face is on T-shirts and there are references to him in rap songs, but it doesn't really reach a level where political action takes off from. These iconic figures have lost their radical dimension. They've been stripped away of what made them radical and controversial. They've come to be seen as consensual, unless we work to make them nonconventional again, to put them back in their context. And that's the academic work that needs to be done today.[33]

Ndiaye said he thought that "France has a lot to learn from other countries, like the US, where there is a long history of political fights, organizations, and nonwhite activism."[34] Speaking to this point, Ndiaye quotes the famed American sociologists Michael Omi and Howard Winant in his book, *La Condition Noire:* "Pour combattre le racism, il faut preter attention a la race"—to fight racism, one must take race into account.[35] Despite its many challenges, that has been the legal, and to a lesser extent, political principle underlying US policy since the civil rights movement.

The French republican dream evaporated before Carlos Moore's eyes in February of 1965, when the French government refused entry to Malcolm X. At a protest rally, Moore delivered a speech at Maubert Mutualité, where Malcolm had spoken in November. "We want the French Government to hear this denunciation tonight because France has always been considered a sanctuary," he said, "a liberal country of little racism—many blacks in the United States think that France is a better place to live and they come here because they hear that there is no racism in France like there is in the United States."[36] Moore went on to rebuke the facade of "equality, fraternity" in France, as Malcolm was forced to fly to London and abandon his hopes of securing an organizational foothold on the Continent. He would never return to Europe again.

Organizations such as CRAN have had varying degrees of success in advancing the struggle for racial equality in France. As Ndiaye notes, "It hasn't become the organization it wanted to be. It's still an elitist group working in Paris with some ties outside of Paris. It has not developed into the type of national organization that we wanted it to become."[37] Part of the difficulty faced by racial, or so-called identity, organizations in France is their sense of inherent illegitimacy. "There's a French exceptionalism in terms of race," Ndiaye continues. "We're proud to say that interracial marriage isn't a problem ... but between that and saying that French society doesn't have any problems with race is another thing."[38] Malcolm would mock this colorblind racial ideal when he was denied entry to France in

FIGURE 6.2 "La prière a l'heure de l'apéro," Collection Salut Barbès. (Bruno Lemesle)

1965. "Maybe my plane got mixed up and I was in South Africa, in the wrong country. And I told them 'This couldn't be Paris! It must be Johannesburg.'"[39]

The French artist Bruno Lemesle captured the complexity of French identity politics and its uneasy place in French society in a photograph taken in Barbès (figure 6.2). The photo depicts a young Parisian woman kneeling alongside the edge of a rooftop in the largely North African section of town. She has immediately under her head, perched inches before the roof's edge, a glass of red wine. She appears to be blonde and decidedly curious. To her left and just right of center to the viewer, there appears the familiar image of the Sacré Coeur, the gleaming white basilica, hovering over the protagonists. And, then directly below it, and the woman, we see a street scene. It is of Muslims making their afternoon prayer. The men are in various stages of standing, kneeling, and fully crouched prayer. The patterns of prayer rugs can be seen, while there is no visible evidence of a mosque. Shot in black and white, the photograph can be read— perhaps like the larger mise en scène of racial and religious politics in France—any number of ways. Perhaps Lemesle has shown us the essence of French cosmopolitanism—one religious tradition, old and sitting upon a hill, remains protected, even revered, if no longer the symbol of religious devotion in a highly secularized society; another religious tradition, less revered by the general public, nevertheless, is active, public, and routine. The Church and the Street are subjects of worship—but not compulsively so, as the young woman and her wine convey perhaps the preeminent virtue of French culture—the right to indulge one's tastes artfully in daily life. This is a picture of Islam, Christianity, and the secular, coexisting, without fear, without judgment. It is simply "Prayer Time at the Hour of the Aperitif"—the photograph's title.[40]

The less charitable interpretation is that of division—the woman is alone on the rooftop, after all. She is apart from the crowd. What must she be thinking? Are those streets no longer hers? Is she forced to the margins of society, as so many on the far Right of France would suggest today?[41] She is in this interpretation torn between the old France of religious piety and tradition and the new one—a nation of religiously observant immigrants, Muslims no less—whose worship becomes a form of public spectacle. She is forced to the rooftops, with the rest of proudly secular and republican French society. However one views the photograph, it is likely to reveal more about one's own politics and vision of French society than anything Lemesle might have intended. It is to be sure, a picture of Western Europe that Malcolm X was just being introduced to, as the first shades of its coloring were coming into view. But what could we learn about Malcolm and his virtue by revisiting his encounter with a Europe undergoing such sweeping transformation?

Malcolm's Europe: Then and Now

It has long been suspected that Malcolm was barred from visiting Paris a second time by the US government, out of fear that he would potentially weaken support for US policies in France and its former colonies. The Cold War aims of America ran directly counter to Malcolm's own, and for this reason his efforts to speak out against racial discrimination at home were seen as an unwelcome counternarrative to US foreign policy imperatives in Europe and beyond. As far back as 1956, the United States Information Agency (USIA) had been conducting public opinion polls of "treatment of Negroes in the U.S." In 1956, 65 percent of French respondents had an unfavorable view, topped only by Great Britain, whose respondents had a 66 percent unfavorability rating, and Norway, which came in at 82 percent.[42] Today, the Cold War has been replaced with a "War on Terror," but the US is no less concerned with its international image. As a 2008 *New York Times* article pointed out, "American embassies [in France] have been instructed to court second- and third-generation immigrants from North Africa, Turkey or Pakistan," for the purpose of educating them about the benefits of American cultural diversity.[43] The program has had its detractors, as the *Times* noted:

> After a Paris newspaper ran a front-page story last month listing a few cultural projects financed by the U.S. Embassy, indignation erupted. "The CIA in the suburbs" read the banner during a documentary by the public broadcaster France 2. The left-leaning magazine Marianne warned of an "American takeover of Arabs and blacks."[44]

It is no wonder that the United States has been interested in changing the dynamic of minority French perceptions of America. As Patrick Lozès, the founder of CRAN, and a candidate for France's presidency in 2012 noted, in 2008, there was only "one black member representing continental France in the National Assembly among 555 members; no continental French senators out of some 300; only a handful of mayors out of some 36,000, and none from the poor Paris suburbs."[45] Pap Ndiaye put it in comparative perspective: "We in France are, in terms of race, where we were in terms of gender 40 years ago."[46]

The situation with regard to Islam's presence in France can be said to be conceived as even more dire. The 2005 uprisings in France's suburbs remain the subject of much debate about the value and future of the Republic's immigration policies. Robert Leiken expresses the imminent sense of crisis caused by these episodes in his unfortunately titled, if otherwise important book, *Europe's Angry Muslims*:

> If it was not an Islamist intifada, what was it? For eighteen days, immigration's offspring had rioted in the *banlieues* of Paris, Lyon, Toulouse, Lille, Nice, and other French cities. 87,00 automobiles and 30,000 trashcans were burned; 140 buses stoned; 255 schools, 233 public buildings, 100 post offices, and more than 20 houses of worship damaged; 200 million euros' worth of property sacked (80 percent public); 4700 individuals arrested; and 597 imprisoned (including 108 minors). France had never seen riots lasting so long or covering such large tracts of the country.[47]

Leiken goes on to emphasize the economic disparities and discrimination affecting immigrant workers in France, connecting the rebellions in France to "the sense of discrimination that fired the American civil rights movement and the riots James Baldwin described."[48] In the nearly fifty years since Malcolm X visited Paris, there remains little to no organizational or leadership-driven effort to unite the claims of France's racial and religious minorities into a coherent voice for equality. As Ndiaye told me, "In France, people talk about communitarianism and identity politics. This is really a negative word. It insinuates people pulling away from French republican values. It is a very powerful way to delegitimize a person without looking at what they have to say. The same goes for Muslims."[49]

It was not so much Muslims, per se, but rather Algerians who defined the modern French experience with the "Other." Three years before Malcolm arrived in Paris, as many as perhaps two hundred or more Algerians were murdered at the hands of the city's police forces, many of them on the single night of October 17, 1961. Their deaths—many never noted in official records—a product of their bodies being dumped into the Seine—were almost immediately discounted, minimized, and all but forgotten over the years. The republican principle dies hard—especially when history runs its underlying superficiality aground. As Jim House and Neil MacMaster point out in their meticulous study of the 1961 killings, "There was, officially, no massacre on 17 October, nor had there been any state terror: the dominant narratives remained in place in France."[50] Malcolm's presence in France had, and no doubt would have continued to have, drawn sharp contrasts with French republican principles in speech as opposed to those administered in practice. While he directed his expert gaze at national racially incentivized hypocrisy in the United States, it was now also fixed upon the capitals of Europe. Malcolm was not necessarily being provocative in Paris when, during his November 1964 speech, he declined to uphold Frederick Douglass and Sojourner Truth alone as preeminent examples of those fighting for racial justice. "Douglass was great," he said in response to a question from a member of the audience. "I would rather have been taught about Toussaint L'Ouverture. We need to be taught about people who fought, who bled for freedom, and made others bleed."[51]

Malcolm's logical progression from questions of race in America to anticolonial struggles abroad presented a rhetorical powder-keg for both American and European states interested in maintaining stability at home. If anything, as Paul Gilroy instructs, the national defense of the colonial enterprise served this purpose, as the "retelling [of] these colonial stories projects the imperial nation as the primary victim rather than the principle beneficiary of its vanished colonial dominance."[52] The stories Malcolm wished to tell—in Paris, in Oxford, and throughout the rest of Western Europe—were those of the colonized. It is an underlying reason why Malcolm was such an effective storyteller in evoking images and archetypes from American slavery. He told their stories so that whites—and perhaps more importantly, blacks—would never forget.

Malcolm's efforts in Europe were also directed toward developing closer ties between the black West Indian, South Asian, and African communities he encountered. The emergent unity of purpose he found in Smethwick, England, shaped by housing discrimination and other forms of racism, was not long-lived. The black and Asian populations of Great Britain have in many ways diverged over the past fifty years, with the black population still in many respects struggling for economic justice. My journey to Smethwick bore this out as today's Midland area remains diverse, if in some respects still divided. As I arrived in Smethwick, I began to search for Marshall Street, the street Malcolm visited in February of 1965. I soon came upon a tall, striking man who introduced himself to me as Jonathan Mill. He was curious about why I was looking for Marshall Street when I explained the nature of my research. "What is all this talk, man, of Malcolm being gay?" he began. I soon learned his family was from St. Kitts. He and I shared a brief exchange about Malcolm's importance. "I don't know," I explained diplomatically. "I think people are seeing all kinds of things in Malcolm these days." I got directions and soon departed but not before getting a sense from Jonathan that the black community in Smethwick remains well aware of Malcolm X.

The directions were apparently mysterious to me and I was walking a great distance. I was clearly in a South Asian Muslim section of town. The billboards and shop windows proved as much as I passed signs for "Desi Builders," "Punjabi Roots," "Smethwick Asian Funerals," and black barber shops next to stores proclaiming, "We Sell African Foods Here." There were an innumerable number of Muslim sweet shops to boot. After what seemed like a good mile or more, I came across the Smethwick Heritage Centre, where I stopped in, hoping this time I'd get directions I could follow. The small Center was a veritable museum of Smethwick memorabilia. Old gear and clothing from the bygone days of industrial Smethwick were on display. The faces in the photos on the walls were of white shopkeepers and schoolgirls and foundrymen. It reminded me of Bethlehem, Pennsylvania, nostalgia for the heyday of Bethlehem Steel. An older gentleman working in the museum handed me a brochure as I looked around. "Discover the true Smethwick," it read. After my brief tour I went about asking for Marshall Street. He and his wife spent the next fifteen minutes trying to explain which bus to take to get there. They even drew me a map that I couldn't figure out if my life depended on it. I thanked them and headed out, but was quickly asked by the older man, "What are you looking for Marshall Street for?" Knowing the Pandora's box of history—1964, Malcolm X, "Nigger Neighbor," and all of that, I realized it was best to duck out before I lost another precious hour. "Oh," I said, "I'm just doing a little research on the town."

"I used to live over on Marshall Street," the gentleman told me. Doing the quick math in my head, I imagined he might have been thirty five or so back when Malcolm visited. "Is that right?" I said, and then a quick "Cheers!" before ducking out.

When I finally got to Marshall Street, I knew I was in the right place. There was the familiar brick wall—I remembered it from BBC footage of Malcolm's visit. This other area I recognized—it looked like the place where Malcolm took a memorable photo standing in front of the Marshall Street sign, wearing a black Russian hat and showing a stern countenance (figure 6.3). A plaque commemorating his visit to the town had been erected not that long ago by black residents, seeking to keep the link between their city and Malcolm alive.

FIGURE 6.3 Malcolm X in Smethwick, England, protesting against anti-black and anti-Asian housing discrimination. (*Birmingham Mail*)

The blue disc plaque bears the name "Malcolm X" above a short statement. Below the statement is the single word—"Recognize." The statement reads, "International civil rights campaigner, advocated desegregated housing in Smethwick with his visit to Marshall Street in 1965."[53]

As I finally turned onto Marshall Street, I was struck by the small but very well-appointed homes I saw. The address signs bore the surnames of people from South Asia. There were a number of doctor's and dentist's offices along either side of the street, and the occasional BMW, Mercedes Benz, and Audi, parked conspicuously throughout the neighborhood. "The thing I notice," Christie Davies told me months later when reflecting upon the legacy of immigration in Great Britain over the last fifty years, "is the huge Hindu and Sikh success on the one hand and the Muslims on the other." The descendants of West Indian immigrants have fared even less well,

Christie observed, making Malcolm's strong desire for a unified black-Asian-Muslim struggle a casualty of uneven postindustrial development in England. "Blacks have not had the same degree of social mobility," Christie noted. "Look at it this way, if I go down to the hospital, if I see Asian faces, it'd be so ordinary, I wouldn't think anything of it," he said. "But you don't see many black faces in the hospitals."[54] Paul Gilroy explains it this way: "We certainly get to see more black people in the dreamscape of advertising, on television, and on the sports field," he notes, "though not in Parliament, the police service, or the judge's bench." Leaving Smethwick, back on my train to Oxford, I thought about Jonathan Mill, the first Smethwick resident I encountered, tall, black, and a devotee of Malcolm. His name couldn't help but conjure up thoughts of John Stuart Mill, the enlightened theorist on democracy. And I thought of Smethwick, located in Britain's "Black Country," so named for the smoke and coal that made the region famous. Soon the train was producing a flash of countryside as the windows' images, as if from a projection, seemed to run from Smethwick; seemed to run away from 1965.

On May 24, 2012, I took my seat in the Oxford Union debate hall. I was curious to learn how much the Union had retained of the old days, the procedures, rituals, and spirit from what I could glean from my readings and viewing of BBC footage from the 1964 debate. It took some doing, as I was not a member, but the Union president, Isabel Ernst, graciously granted me permission to attend the debate as her guest. I couldn't help but think of how the world at large, let alone the world at Oxford, had changed since Malcolm had been there. A woman president—and a German, no less; how decidedly far removed from 1964 indeed. As the now air-conditioned hall slowly filled up, I soon discerned that not only was the current Union president a woman, but so too was the treasurer (a Russian) and the secretary. The lone male officer I could make out was the librarian. Glancing around, I quickly gathered that other than me, there was but one other person of African descent in the hall—a woman sitting on the left side of the debate hall. Perhaps it was an off night.

Like most elite institutions, Oxford University has become very interested in improving its image with respect to the diversity of its student population. The 2011 statistics for BMEs—Black and Minority Ethnic students—shows a 20 percent overall presence at the university.[55] There's no mistaking that today's Oxford is significantly more diverse along not only racial, but also gender and socioeconomic, lines than it was just twenty years ago, let alone a half-century ago. But the themes and issues of the Union remain constant, to be sure. "This House believes force can be used in defending human rights," was the motion the night of my visit. It wasn't "extremism in the defense of liberty," but it was close. And like Malcolm's defense of extremism, the defenders of "force" lost in this debate. Of course, the changes in technology were present. Despite the fact that Union rules stipulate that "Members are reminded that they should not use mobile telephones in the chamber at any time," at least one of the speakers read her notes for the debate off of her smartphone.[56] In a world where people can watch Parliament on C-SPAN, the allure of the Union debates—where ordinary people could get a sense of what it was like to see the House of Commons in action—is not what it once was. It would be far easier today for Malcolm to get his views out more readily to the broader public, indeed, to the world. But in a sense, the aura and mystery of Malcolm X, which no doubt contributed to his success as a leader and a speaker, would suffer from the saturation of words and images common to today's politics. And yet perhaps Malcolm's forceful character and personality, as well as his deep commitment to principles of basic fairness and justice, would somehow filter out into the people he would be trying to reach.

In time, the false choice between the "unchanging" and "elusive" Malcolms grew before me, as I pondered the demands the past have placed upon the present. What we want Malcolm X to be today says more about our politics, and perhaps our own insecurities, than it may about Malcolm X as a person. This was the wisdom in Carlos Moore's hesitance to prophesy over Malcolm's lost future. Like the

Lemesle photograph, we read into Malcolm our own projections about the nature of change in our world. But still there remained the question of virtue and what to make of Malcolm at Oxford, a question that went beyond the purely historical confines of the Oxford debate.

The thought drew me back to my conversation with Tariq Ali, one that I've come to accept best captures who and what Malcolm was at Oxford and beyond. "I talked to a friend who told me what Hugh MacDiarmid said about Malcolm X after having met him at Oxford," Ali told me. I paused, wondering what the one-time Scottish Nationalist thought of the one-time Black Nationalist. "Do you know the two words MacDiarmid used to describe Malcolm X?" Ali asked, teasingly.

I let the question hang in the air for a few beats. "Tell me," I relented.

"Authentic revolutionary."[57]

Epilogue: "Defiance"

Jesse Jackson was tired. And hungry. James Peterson, the new director of Africana Studies at Lehigh University, had brought Reverend Jackson to Lehigh to deliver a talk and to meet and greet faculty and students during Black History Month. It had been a long day. "Where's James?" Jackson joked. "You're trying to starve me, feeding me this cheese and crackers." There were many in line wanting to meet Jackson during the reception, and James, familiar with my project, ushered me over to the reverend.

"Saladin here is working on a book on Malcolm X," James noted, introducing us.

"I was wondering, Reverend, if you'd ever met Malcolm?" I asked.

Jackson proceeded to tell the story of having driven from Greensboro, North Carolina, to Harlem Mosque Number 7 in an effort to meet Malcolm. Jackson was in his late teens at the time. "He wasn't there. He was out of town," Jackson recalled.

I was struck by the effort he took to meet Malcolm. In the age before cell phones, Jackson simply drove on faith. Malcolm must have had an incredible aura about him to inspire such an act. But then Jackson offered a response to an unasked question about Malcolm, one I was struck by.

"Malcolm and Dr. King—really, they shouldn't even be mentioned in the same sentence," he offered. Internally, I was floored, but I pivoted as best I could. After Jackson talked briefly about Dr. King having the "superior vision," I asked, "Well, what in your estimation was Malcolm's contribution to the struggle?" Without missing a beat he gave it.

"Defiance," he said.[1]

I've weighed that response since and remain intrigued by how much Malcolm's political thought—indeed the depth and power of his analyses not only on race, but on politics, history, and American culture, has languished under the weight of his role as *provocateur*. I understood immediately, why Jackson, a close lieutenant of Dr. King's, might see *Malcolmania* as a kind of cultural assault upon the legacy of not only King, but the entirety of the nonviolent struggle for freedom that defined the civil rights movement. This sentiment continues to trouble a good deal of the independent work done on Malcolm, as it demands some kind of explanation for thinking about and studying him on his own terms. And yet interest in Malcolm seems to draw from a bottomless well. Still, that interest hasn't resolved the compelling, but often premature, thought that somehow, we already know him.

I, too, suffered from this. I was part of the generation of young black males that embraced Malcolm; embraced him in word, image, and deed. I became Saladin Malik Ambar, as so many of my generation took on new names—if not because of Malcolm, then at least with his ghostly assistance. And we took to reading what Malcolm read, tried to fast like Malcolm fasted, tried to imagine ourselves as tall, as beautiful, and as unafraid as he was. Many of us made knowing Malcolm a kind of vocation. And yet, as recently as two years ago, I was teaching black political thought to undergraduates at Lehigh and was struck by how unfamiliar I was with Malcolm's speech at Oxford. And in a sense, I was struck by the salience of not only his perspective there concerning race, but also his views on the emerging postcolonial world, still taking shape, now fifty years later. Oxford, I've come to accept, humbles our best efforts to apprehend Malcolm in many ways, because it reminds us just how rapidly he was developing; how catching Malcolm was like trying to catch daylight. The shadows it casts are ever-changing. We mistake our sameness for its constancy. This, I am convinced, is the source of Malcolm's boundless attractiveness over the years. He is at once familiar and enigmatic.

Jackson had hit on something with "defiance." But I think it was and is far more an open-ended, rather than definitive, term with regard to Malcolm. As it was at Oxford, it retains an accessibility and power beyond race and time. Malcolm's defiance holds not just visceral but also intellectual appeal for African Americans to be sure, and blacks more broadly, without question. But Oxford's defiant reach extends to Asians, Muslims, the poor, the embattled, and all of those oppressed, regardless of race. Malcolm at Oxford indeed universalizes black anguish—not just black aspirations, as is suggested in so many treatises on the life and politics of Martin Luther King Jr. But anguish is no less real than hope, defiance no less strategic than consensus. Malcolm's appeal to his audience at Oxford to "approach extremism not as an American or a European or an African or an Asian, but as a human being," is a powerful and ultimately unique call for recognition of black humanity. It is so precisely because it asks whites, and the world at large, not to embrace black *love*, but rather, black *anger*. It may be easier to legitimate love, but coming to grips with well-earned anger requires a level of empathy, which in turn demands a kind of earnestness that may prove more healing. To deny human fury is to deny the humanity of those who harbor it. Malcolm at Oxford wasn't seeking to make black fury permanent; he was seeking to render it immaterial by making its basic universality legitimate. He did so with his own rising belief that whites could in fact get to black humanity through this difficult door. But that door was hard to open for a reason—it had been sealed shut by centuries of presumptive white supremacy. To open it, whites were going to have to destroy something dark within themselves, and not merely accept the love and passivity from the souls of black folk.

In one sense, the world of those who "knew" Malcolm is coming to a close, but in another, it is just opening. The Oxford moment introduced him to an entirely new population of thinkers, scholars, and activists. This new world continues to grow, and in it Malcolm will undoubtedly take on new meaning. There has long been a sense from his detractors that Malcolm has been overappraised, if not overrated, over these nearly fifty years since his death. He left no legislation, no philosophical treatise, no building, no organization. Having been asked many times over the past two years, "What is the legacy of Malcolm?," "What is the legacy of Oxford?," I can only suggest the answer is far more difficult than the question. On one hand, merely asking the question places the questioner in the passive role in both history and the present; as if we the living, to invoke an ironic turn of phrase from Jefferson, have no authority over shaping the meaning of the past, or in defining the question of legacy through our own actions. My own answer instead forces me to turn to Hugh MacDiarmid's two-word response in describing the essence of Malcolm—a response that should both haunt and inspire, as it admittedly did for me in writing this book. What two words would I want to define my life, and my life's work? Few, if any of us, may ever be said to fulfill the legacy of Malcolm as MacDiarmid so succinctly described it—"authentic revolutionary." But our own two indeterminate words serve their own purpose, as I imagine Malcolm would want them to. Not to make his legacy come to life. But to be fearless in bringing to life our own. By whatever means necessary.

THE OXFORD ADDRESS AT THE
OXFORD UNION DEBATE

MALCOLM X

December 3, 1964

Oxford Union Society President, Eric Anthony Abrahams

It is with great pleasure that I call upon Mr. Malcolm X to speak fifth, in favor of the motion
[*Extended applause*].

Malcolm X

Mr. Chairman, tonight is the first night that I've ever had an opportunity to be as near to conservatives [*Laughter*] as I am. And the speaker who preceded me—First, I want to thank you for the invitation to come here to the Oxford Union. The speaker who preceded me is one of the best excuses that I know to prove our point concerning the *necessity*, sometimes, of extremism, in defense of liberty, why it is no vice, and why moderation in the pursuit of justice is no virtue. I don't say that about him personally [*Laughter*], but that *type* is the—[*Laughter, applause*].

He's right, X is not my real name, [*Laughter*] but if you study history you'll find why no black man in the Western Hemisphere knows his real name. Some of his ancestors kidnapped our ancestors from Africa, and took us into the Western Hemisphere and sold us there. And our names were stripped from us and so today we don't know who we really are. I am one of those who admit it and so I just put X up there to keep from wearing his name. [*Laughter*]

And as far as this apartheid charge that he attributed to me is concerned, evidently he has been misinformed. I don't believe in any form of apartheid, I don't believe in any form of segregation, I don't believe in any form of racialism. But at the same time, I don't endorse a person as being right just because his skin is white, and ofttimes when you find people like this—I mean that type [*Laughter*], when a man whom they have been taught is below them has the nerve or firmness to question some of their philosophy or some of their conclusions, usually they put that label on us, a label that is only designed to project an image which the public will find distasteful.

I am a Muslim, [*Short applause*] if there is something wrong with that then I stand condemned. My religion is Islam; I believe in Allah, I believe in Muhammad as the apostle of Allah, I believe in brotherhood, of *all* men, but I don't believe in brotherhood with anybody who's not ready to practice brotherhood with our people. [*Applause*] I don't believe in brotherhood—[*More applause*]. I just take time to make these few things clear because I find that one of the tricks of the West, and I imagine my good friend or at least that type [*Laughter*] is from the West, one of the tricks of the West is to use or create images.

They create images of a person who doesn't go along with their views and then they make certain that this image is distasteful, and then anything that person has to say from there on, from there on in, is rejected. And this is a policy that has been practiced pretty well, pretty much by the West, it perhaps would have been practiced by others had they been in power, but during recent centuries the West has been in power, they've created the images, and they've used these images quite skillfully and quite successfully, that's why today we need a little extremism in order to straighten a very nasty situation out, or a very *extremely* nasty situation out. [*Laughter*]

I think the only way one can really determine whether or not extremism in defense of liberty is justified, is not to approach it as an American or a European or an African or an Asian, but as a human being. If we look upon it as different types immediately we begin to think in terms of extremism being good for one and bad for another, or bad for one and good for another. But if we look upon it, if we look upon ourselves as human beings, I doubt that anyone will deny that extremism, in defense of liberty, the liberty of *any* human being isn't a vice. Anytime anyone is enslaved, or in any way deprived of his liberty, if that person is a human being, as far as I am concerned he is justified to resort to whatever methods necessary to bring about his liberty again. [*Applause*]

But most people [*Malcolm chuckles*] usually think in terms of extremism, as something that is relative, related to someone whom they know or something that they've heard of, I don't think they look upon extremism by itself, or all alone. They apply it to something. A good example—and one of the reasons that this can't be too well understood today—many people who have been in positions of power in the past don't realize that the power, the centers of power, are changing. When you're in a position of power for a long time you get used to using your yardstick, and you take it for granted that because you've forced your yardstick upon others, that everyone is still using the same yardstick. So that your definition of extremism usually applies to everyone, but nowadays times are changing, and the center of power is changing. People in the past who weren't in a position to have a yardstick or use a yardstick of their own are using their own yardstick now. You use one and they use another. In the past when the oppressor had one stick and the oppressed used that same stick, today the oppressed are sort of shaking the shackles and getting yardsticks of their own, so when they say extremism they don't mean what you do, and when you say extremism you don't mean what *they* do. There are entirely two different meanings. And when this is understood I think you can better understand why those who are using methods of extremism are being driven to them.

A good example is the Congo. When the people who are in power want to use again, create an image, to justify something that's bad, they use the press. And they'll use the press to create a humanitarian image, for a devil, or a devil image for a humanitarian. They'll take a person who's a victim of the crime, and make it appear he's the criminal, and they'll take the criminal and make it appear that he's the victim of the crime. And the Congo situation is one of the best examples that I can cite right now to point this out. The Congo situation is a nasty example of how a country because it is in power, can take its press and make the world accept something that's absolutely criminal. They take American trained—they take pilots that they say are "American trained," and this automatically lends respectability to them [*Laughter*], and then they will call them "anti-Castro Cubans," and that's supposed to add to their respectability [*Laughter*], and eliminate that fact that they're dropping bombs on villages where they have no defense whatsoever against such planes, blowing to bits black women, Congolese women, Congolese children, Congolese babies, this is extremism, but it is never referred to as extremism because it is endorsed by the West, it is financed by America, it's made respectable by America, and that kind of extremism is never labeled as extremism. Because it's not extremism in defense of liberty, and if it is extremism in defense of liberty as this type just pointed out, it is extremism in defense of liberty for the wrong type of people. [*Applause*] I am not advocating that kind of extremism, that's cold-blooded murder. But the press is used to make that cold-blooded murder appear as an act of humanitarianism.

They take it one step farther and get a man named Tshombe, who is a murderer, they refer to him as the Premier, or the Prime Minister of the Congo, to lend respectability to him, he's actually the murderer of the rightful Prime Minister of the Congo, they never mention this. [*Applause*] I'm not for extremism in defense of that kind of liberty, or that kind of activity. They take this man, who's a *murderer*, and the world recognizes him as a *murderer*, but they make him the Prime Minister, he becomes a *paid* murderer, a paid killer, who is propped up by American dollars. And to show the degree to which he is a paid killer the first thing he does is go to South Africa and hire more killers and bring them into the Congo. They give them the glorious name of mercenary, which means a hired killer, not someone that's killing for some kind of patriotism or some kind of ideal, but a man who is a *paid* killer, a *hired* killer. And one of the leaders of them is right from this country here, and he's glorified as a soldier of fortune when he's shooting down little black women and black babies and black children. I'm not for that kind of extremism, I'm for the kind of extremism that those who are being *destroyed* by those bombs and *destroyed* by those hired killers, are able to put forth to thwart it. They will risk their lives at any cost, they will sacrifice their lives at any cost, against that kind of criminal activity. I'm for the kind of extremism that the freedom fighters in the Stanleyville regime are able to display against these hired killers, who are actually using some of my tax dollars that I have to pay up in the United States, to finance that operation over there. We're not for that kind of extremism.

And again I think you must point out that the real criminal over there is the or rather one of the [*Laughs to himself*]—one of those who are very much involved as accessories to the crime is the press. Not so much your press, but the American press which has tricked your press into repeating what they have invented. [*Laughter and applause*] But I was reading in one of the English papers this morning, I think it's a paper called The Express [*Laughter and applause*], and it gave a very clear account [*Laughter*], of the type of criminal activity that has been carried on by the mercenaries that are being paid by United States tax dollars. And it showed where they were killing Congolese, whether they were from the central government or the Stanleyville government, it didn't make any difference to them, they just killed them. [*Laughter*] And they had it fixed where those who had been processed had to wear a white bandage around their head, and any Congolese that they saw without their white bandage, they killed them. And this is clearly pointed out in the English papers. If they had printed it last week there would have been an outcry and no one would have allowed the Belgians and the United States and the others who are in cahoots with each other, to carry on the criminal activity that they did in the Congo, which I doubt anybody in the world, not even your *Oxford* will accept, not even my friend. [*Laughter*]

Interjection

Inaudible…

Malcolm X

Yes…

Speaker

I wonder what exactly what sort of extremism you would consider the killing of missionaries? [Members of audience: *"Hear, hear!" Applause*].

Malcolm X

I'd call it the type of extremism that was involved when America dropped the bomb on Hiroshima and killed 80,000 people, or over 80,000 people, men, women, children, everything. It was an act of war. I'd call it the same kind of extremism that happened when England dropped bombs on German cities and Germans dropped bombs on English cities. It was an act of war, and the Congo situation is *war*, and when you call it war, then anybody that dies, they die a death that is justified. But those who are, [*Some in audience cry: "No! For shame!"*] but those who are in the Stanleyville regime, sir, are defending their country, those who are coming in are invading their country. And some of the refugees that were questioned on television in this city a couple of days ago pointed out that had the paratroopers not come in they doubted that they would have been molested, they weren't being molested until the paratroopers came in. [*Applause*]

I don't encourage any act of murder nor do I glorify in anybody's death, but I do think that when the white public uses its press to magnify the fact that there are the lives of white hostages at stake, they don't say "hostages," every paper says "*white* hostages." They give me the impression that they attach more importance to a white hostage and a white death, than they do the death of a human being, despite the color of his skin. [*Prolonged applause*] I feel forced to make that point clear, that I'm not for any indiscriminate killing, nor does the death of so many people go by me without creating some kind of emotion. But I think that white people are making the mistake, and if they read their own newspapers they will have to agree that they in clear cut language make a distinction between the type of dying according to the color of the skin. And when you begin to think in terms of death being death, no matter what type of human being it is, then we will all probably be able to sit down as human beings and get rid of this extremism and moderation. But as long as the situation exists as it is, we're going to need some extremism, and I think some of you will need some moderation too.

So why would such an act in the Congo, which is so clearly criminal, be condoned? It's condoned primarily because it has been glorified by the press and has been made to look beautiful, and therefore the world automatically sanctions it. And this is the role that the press plays, if you study back in history different wars, always the press, whenever a country that's in power wants to step in unjustly and invade someone else's property, they use the press to make it appear that the area that they are about to invade is filled with savages, or filled with people who have gone berserk, or they are raping white women, molesting nuns, they use the same old tactic year in and year out.

Now there was a time when the dark world, people with dark skin, would believe anything that they saw in the papers that originated in Europe. But today, no matter *what* is put in the paper, they stop and look at it two or three times and try and figure out what is the motive of the writer. And usually they can determine what the motive of the writer is. The powers that be use the press to give the devil an angelic image and give the image of the devil to the one who's really angelic. They make oppression and exploitation and *war* actually look like an act of humanitarianism. This is not the kind of extremism that I support or that I go along with.

One of the reasons that I think it's necessary for me to clarify my own point, personally, I was in a conversation with a student here on the campus yesterday [*Short laughter and applause*], and she, after we were, I think we had coffee or something, dinner—there were several of us—I have to add that in for those minds of yours that run astray. [*Laughter*] And she asked me, she told me that, "Well, I'm surprised that you're not what I expected," and I said what do you mean? [*Laughter*] And she said, "Well, I was looking for your horns" [*Laughter*], and so I told her I have them, but I keep them hidden [*Laughter*], unless someone draws them out. As my friend, or that type, it takes certain *types* to draw them out. [*Laughter*]

And this is actually true, usually when a person is looked upon as an extremist, anything that person does in your eyesight is extreme. On the other hand, if a person is looked upon as conservative, just about anything they do is conservative. And this comes again through the manipulating of images. What they want you to think—that a certain area or a certain person or a certain group is extremist, or rather is involved in actions of extremism—the first thing they do is project that person in the image of an extremist. And then anything that he does from then on is extreme, you know, it doesn't make any difference whether it is right or wrong, as far as you're concerned if the image is wrong, whatever they do is wrong. And this has been done by the Western press, and also by the American press, and it has been picked up by the English press and the European press. Whenever any black man in America shows signs of an uncompromising attitude, against the injustices that he experiences daily, and shows no tendency whatsoever to deal or compromise with it, then the American press begins to project that person as a radical and extremist, somebody who's irresponsible, or as a rabble-rouser, or someone who use—who doesn't rationalize in dealing with the problem.

Interjection

I wonder whether you'd consider that you have seen me projected, rather successfully, a quite upsetting image of a "type." [*Members of audience object*]

Malcolm X

It depends on which angle [*Protests from audience*], no let the gentleman bring out his point. It depends on which angle you look at it, sir. I never try and hide what I am. If—

Same Speaker

I am referring to your treatment of the previous speaker.

Malcolm X

You're referring to *my* treatment of the *previous* speaker? [*Extended laughter and applause*] You make my point! [*Laughter*] That as long as a white man does it, it's all right, a black man is supposed to have no feelings [*Protests and more applause*]. But when a black man strikes *back*, he's an extremist, he's supposed to sit passively and have no feelings, be nonviolent, and love his enemy no matter what kind of attack, be it verbal or otherwise, he's supposed to take it. But if he stands up in any way and tries to defend himself [*Laughs to himself followed by laughter and applause*] then he's an extremist. [*Extended applause*]

No, I think that the speaker who preceded me is getting exactly what he asked for. [*Laughter*] My reason for believing in extremism, intelligently directed extremism, extremism in defense of liberty, extremism in quest of justice, is because I firmly believe in my *heart*, that the day that the black man takes an uncompromising step, and realizes that he's within his rights, when his own freedom is being jeopardized, to use any means necessary to bring about his freedom, or put a halt to that injustice, I don't think he'll be by himself.

I live in America where there are only 22 million blacks against probably 160 million whites. One of the reasons that I am in no way reluctant or hesitant to do whatever is *necessary* to see that black people do something to protect themselves, I honestly believe that the day that they do, many whites will have more respect for them, and that there'll be more whites on their side than are now on their side with these little wishy-washy "love-thy-enemy" approach that they've been using up until now. And if I'm wrong, than you are racialists. [*Laughter and extended applause*]

As I said earlier, in my conclusion, I'm a Muslim. I believe in Allah, I believe in Muhammad, I believe in all of the prophets. I believe in fasting, prayer, charity, and that which is incumbent upon a Muslim to fulfill in order to be a Muslim. In April I was fortunate to make the Hajj to Mecca, and went back again in September, to try and carry out my religious functions and requirements, but at the same time that I believe in that religion, I have to point out I'm also an American Negro. And I live in a society whose social system is based upon the castration of the black man, whose political system is based upon castration of the black man, and whose economy is based upon the castration of the black man. A society which in 1964 has more subtle, deceptive, deceitful methods to make the rest of the world think that it's cleaning up its house, while at the same time, the same things are happening to us in 1964 that happened in 1954, 1924, and 1984 [1894].

They came up with what they call a civil rights bill in 1964, supposedly to solve our problem, and after the bill was signed, three civil rights workers were *murdered* in cold blood. And the FBI head, Hoover, admits that they know who did it, they've known ever since it happened, and they've done nothing about it. Civil rights bill down the drain. No matter how many bills pass, black people in that country, where I'm from, still our lives are not worth two cents. And the government has shown its inability, or either its unwillingness to do whatever is necessary to protect life and property where the black American is concerned. So *my* contention is that whenever a people come to the conclusion that the government, which they have supported, proves itself unwilling, or proves itself unable to protect *our* lives and protect *our* property, because we have the wrong color skin, we are not human beings unless we ourselves band together and do whatever, however, whenever, is necessary to see that our lives and our property is protected, and I doubt that any person in here would refuse to do the same thing were he in the same position, or I should say were he in the same condition. [*Extended applause*]

Just one step farther to see if I'm justified in this stance, and I say I'm speaking as a black man from America which is a racist society, no matter how much you hear it talk about democracy it's as racist as South Africa or as racist as Portugal or as racist as any other racialist society on this earth. The only difference between it and South Africa, South Africa preaches separation and practices separation; America preaches integration and practices segregation. This is the only difference, they don't practice what they preach, whereas South Africa practices and preaches the same thing. I have more respect for a man who lets me know where he stands, even if he's wrong, than the one who comes up like an angel and is nothing but a devil. [*Applause*]

The system of government that America has consists of committees, [*Some laughter*] there are sixteen senatorial committees that govern the country and twenty congressional committees. Ten of the sixteen senatorial committees are in the hands of southern racialists, senators who are racialists. Thirteen of the twenty, this is before the last election, I think it is even more so now, ten of the sixteen senatorial committees are in the hands of senators who are southern racialists. Thirteen of the twenty congressional committees were in the hands of southern congressmen who are racialists. Which means out of the thirty-six committees that govern the foreign and domestic direction of that government, twenty-three are in the hands of southern racialists—men who in no way believe in the equality of man. And men who'll do anything within their power to see that the black man never gets to the same seat, or to the same level that they're on. The reason that these men, from that area, have that type of power is because America has a seniority system, and these who have that seniority have been there longer than anyone else because the black people in the areas where they live can't vote. And it is only because the black man is deprived of his vote that puts these men in positions of power that gives them such influence in the government beyond their actual intellectual or political ability, or even beyond the number of people from the areas that they represent.

So we can see, in that country, that no matter what the federal government *professes* to be doing, the power of the federal government lies in these committees and any time a black man or any kind of legislation is proposed to benefit the black man, or give the black man his just due, we find that it is locked up in these committees right here. And when they let something through the committees, usually it is so chopped up and fixed up that by the time it becomes law, it's a law that can't be enforced.

Another example is the Supreme Court's desegregation decision that was handed down in 1954. This is a *law*, and this law—they have not been able to implement this law in New York City or in Boston or in Cleveland or Chicago or the northern cities. And my contention is that any time you have a country, supposedly a democracy, supposedly the "land of the free and the home of the brave," and it can't enforce laws, even in the northern most cosmopolitan and progressive part of it, that will benefit a black man, if *those* laws can't be enforced or *that* law can' be enforced, how much heart do you think we will get when they pass some civil rights legislation which only involves more laws? If they can't enforce *this* law, they'll never enforce those laws.

So my contention is, we are faced with a racialistic society, a society in which they are deceitful, deceptive, and the *only* way we can bring about a change is to speak the language that they understand. The racialist never understands a peaceful language, the racialist never understands the nonviolent language, the racialist has spoken his language to us for four hundred years. We have been the victim of his brutality, we are the ones who face his dogs that tear the flesh from our limbs, only because we want to enforce the Supreme Court decision. We are the ones who have our skulls crushed, not by the Ku Klux Klan, but by *policemen*, only because we want to enforce what they call the Supreme Court decision. We are the ones upon whom water hoses are turned, with pressure so hard that it rips the clothes from our backs, not men, but the clothes from the backs of women and children, you've seen it yourself. Only because we want to enforce what they call the law. Well, any time you live in a society supposedly based upon law and it doesn't enforce its own law, because the color of a man's skin happens to be wrong, then I say those people are justified to resort to any means necessary to bring about justice where the government can't give them justice. [*Extended applause*]

I don't believe in any form of unjustified extremism. But I believe that when a man is exercising extremism, a human being is exercising extremism in defense of liberty for human beings, it's no vice. And when one is moderate in the pursuit of justice for human beings, I say he's a sinner. And I might add [*Laughs to himself*] in my conclusion—in fact, America is one of the best examples, when you read its history, about extremism. Old Patrick Henry said "liberty or death"—that's extreme, very extreme. [*Laughter and applause*]

I read once, passingly, about a man named Shakespeare. I only read about him passingly, but I remember one thing he wrote, that kind of moved me. He put it in the mouth of Hamlet, I think it was, who said: "To be, or not to be." He was in doubt about something. [*Laughter*] "Whether it was nobler in the mind of man, to suffer the slings and arrows of outrageous fortune"—moderation—"or to take up arms against a sea of troubles and by opposing end them."

And I go for that. If you take up arms you'll end it, but if you sit around and wait for the one who is in power to make up his mind that he should end it, you'll be waiting a long time. And in my opinion, the young generation of whites, blacks, browns, whatever else there is, you're living at a time of extremism, a time of revolution, a time when there's got to be a change, people in power have misused it, and now there has to be a change. And a better world has to be built and the only way it's going to be built is with extreme methods. And I for one will join in with *anyone*—I don't care what *color* you are—as long as you want to change this miserable condition that exists on this earth.

Thank you.
[*Extended applause lasts ninety seconds*]

ACKNOWLEDGMENTS

"So, I hear you want to talk to me about Brother Malcolm?" Those were the first words I heard at the outset of my research into the story of Malcolm X at Oxford. They were uttered by the late Manning Marable in his Columbia University office. I had spent months trying to get on his calendar to discuss with him my idea for a book on Malcolm and what sources he thought might be most helpful. I braced myself for the possibility that he'd be what more than a few highly successful academics are like about a subject they care deeply about: territorial and condescending. He was anything but. As we discussed Malcolm's travel in the UK, he handed me three pages of his own, as yet, then unpublished manuscript. "I thought these might be helpful," he said. "This is what I've written on Malcolm in England. I'd give you the whole manuscript but my publisher would have my head," he joked. It was an object lesson in how senior scholars can be infinitely valuable to their erstwhile juniors, through simple acts of humility and generosity. It is a lesson I hope never to forget—and I thank Professor Marable, however unfortunately late, for his kindness and belief in this project.

Funding for travel and other expenses related to this research were provided by numerous entities, and I'd like to thank them. They include the Mellon Foundation, whose grant to Lehigh University's Center for Global Islamic Studies helped me get to Oxford. Robert Rozehnal, who directs the center, has been generous of time, resources, and spirit, in support of this book, and is an invaluable colleague and friend. Likewise, James Peterson, who directs Lehigh's Program in Africana Studies, has been similarly supportive, and I owe both him and Africana Studies a great deal of thanks for funding and its commitment to teaching and research in this vital field within the academy. Thankfully, my department chair, Rick Matthews, and colleagues in political science did not look at me as if I sprung three heads when I suggested that I'd interrupt my research into the presidency and such charismatic figures as Rutherford B. Hayes and Grover Cleveland to write about Malcolm X. In fact, quite the opposite is true—and I'm thankful that I could share all manner of aspects of my research with them unapologetically. In particular, I'd like to thank Janet Laible, whose insights into British politics proved inordinately helpful.

My colleagues across the pond who allowed me to interrupt their schedules to get their insights include Sir David Butler and Stephen Tuck of Oxford University; Phillip Giddings of the University of Reading, and Dr. Farhan Nizami, director of the Oxford Centre for Islamic Studies. I'd also like to thank Rachel Hancock of the Oxfordshire Records Office, Anna Petre of the Oxford University Archives, the staff at the Oxford Union Library, the Oxford Union archivist, Graeme Hall, the staff of the Bodleian Library, Hazel Waters and Jenny Bourne—and the entire staff of the Institute of Race Relations in London; Sara Denman and the staff of BBC/Thought Equity, Jeff Walden of the BBC Written Archives, and countless others in the United Kingdom who assisted me along the way.

My research of Malcolm X's time in Paris could not have been undertaken without the assistance in both research and translation of period texts and French news accounts by my research assistant Colleen Casey. I'd also like to thank Pap Ndiaye who was very generous with his time and insights, Monique Y. Wells of Entrée to Black Paris, Sophie Nellis of Context Paris, the staff of L'Institute du Monde Arabe, Jean-Marc Bombeau of L'Echo Musée, along with my friend and colleague at Lehigh University and resident expert in all things Parisian, John Savage. I must also thank my friend and colleague John Pettegrew, who read the manuscript in its entirety, taking valuable time from his own research, to offer insights and suggestions. I'd also like to thank Dalena Hunter, librarian for the Carlos Moore Collection at the Ralph J. Bunche Center at UCLA, along with Mark Sawyer, who introduced me to Carlos and shepherded me through the Carlos Moore papers. The staff at the Schomburg Research Center for Black Culture in Harlem also were exceedingly helpful.

In addition to Carlos Moore, I am thankful to those who agreed to be interviewed by me, including Tariq Ali, Christie Davies, Shirley Anderson Fletcher, Pap Ndiaye, and Tim Gopsill. Many others were willing to share with me their perspectives or assistance during this research, including Ilyasah Shabazz, Jesse Jackson, Bruce Kuklick, Michael Hanchard, Desmond King, Chip Hauss, Vincent Wimbush, Jane Junn, Daniel Tichenor, Ted Morgan, Seth Moglen, Britt Langford, Ed Lundeen, Gregory Reed, Candace Cox-Wimberley, and Donnell Mason, my gracious host at Wayne County Community College in Detroit. I'd be remiss if I didn't thank my agent Geri Thoma, who thought the story of Malcolm X at Oxford Union worth fighting for. I am also thankful to David McBride of Oxford University Press for his encouragement and support. And, not to be forgotten, Sarah Rosenthal of OUP, who pushed to make the writing herein as strong as possible.

Finally, I am eternally grateful to my wife Carmen and our children, Gabby, Luke, and Daniel. The last two years I have been away more times than either they, or I, care to remember. It is good to be home.

NOTES

Chapter 1

1. The first debate was held the year after the Union was formed. The question was "Was the revolution under Cromwell to be attributed to the tyrannical conduct of Charles, or to the democratic spirit of the times?" The doors to the debate hall, like much of the physical layout of the hall, were designed to evoke the House of Commons. Fiona Graham, *Playing at Politics: An Ethnography of the Oxford Union* (Edinburgh: Dunedin Academic Press, 2005), 25, 41–42.

2. "I really don't like wearing tails," Malcolm demurred to his host Eric Abrahams, "but if it's going to be any embarrassment to you at all, I'd be happy to wear tails." Jan Carew, *Ghosts in Our Blood: With Malcolm X in Africa, England, and the Caribbean* (Chicago: Lawrence Hill Books, 1994), 73.

3. In 1969 Denis Greenhill went on to become permanent undersecretary at the Foreign Office and head of the Diplomatic Service. Foreign Office Files: The United States of America (FO 371/168485), Microfilm Reel 26, National Archives, Kew, UK (hereafter National Archives). Despatch No. 116, Reference 1824. Confidential despatch, D. A. Greenhill, British Embassy, August 6, 1963.

4. Ibid.

5. Ibid.

6. Harold Macmillan, Letter dated September 5, 1963, National Archives.

7. Dennis Greenhill, Letter from British Embassy in Washington to Foreign Office, July 29, 1963 (FO 371/168485), National Archives.

8. Martin Luther King Jr., *A Testament of Hope: The Essential Writings and Speeches of Martin Luther King, Jr.*, ed. James M. Washington (New York: HarperCollins, 1986), 239.

9. British Ambassador Sir Patrick Dean to British consul in Los Angeles, September 10, 1965 (FO 371/179611), National Archives; emphasis added.

10. The official photograph from the December 3 debate does not hang outside the debate hall. There is a picture displayed of Malcolm and his coparticipants from the debate, a posed shot, hanging on a wall in the Union's main building corridor.

11. "Black Muslim in Oxford," *Oxford Mail*, December 12, 1964.

12. Carew, 41.

13. Eric Abrahams, Letter to Malcolm X, November 27, 1964, the Malcolm X Collection: Papers (1948–1965), Box 3, Speaking Engagements, Schomburg Center for Research in Black Culture, New York Public Library. Malcolm X Collection: Papers (1948–1965), Speaking Engagements, Box 3.

14. Carew, 72.

15. "The Proctors and Politics," *Isis*, week ending October 10, 1964.

16. There is considerable disagreement about how many of these gatherings took place, and precisely how many Oxford students were involved, as will be discussed in chapter 6. Author interviews with Tariq Ali, May 22, 2012, and Shirley Anderson Fletcher, June 19, 2012. See also Carew, 72–73.

17. Berkeley had himself been "sent down" from Cambridge University in the 1920s because of student misbehavior. The BBC broadcast is available through an American company, Thought Equity Motion. BBC broadcast, December 3, 1964.

18. Tariq Ali, *Street Fighting Years: An Autobiography of the Sixties* (New York: Verso, 2005), 104.

19. "Topless Fails to Appear," *Oxford Mail*, December 5, 1964.

20. Ali, 104.

21. Ibid., 106.

22. Judy G. Batson, *Her Oxford* (Nashville: Vanderbilt University Press, 2008), 286.

23. Christopher Hollis, *The Oxford Union* (London: Evans Brothers Limited, 1965), 222.

24. "Coming Out of the Dark Ages," *The Guardian*, June 27, 2007.

25. See Manning Marable on Malcolm's sexuality in *Malcolm X: A Life of Reinvention* (Viking: New York, 2011), 65–66.

26. Ossie Davis, "Eulogy for Malcolm X," in *For Malcolm: Poems on the Life and the Death of Malcolm X*, ed. Dudley Randall and Margaret G. Burroughs (Detroit: Broadside Press, 1969), 121.

27. Vijay Prashad shatters the myth of a racially monolithic Harlem in *Everybody Was Kung Fu Fighting: Afro-Asian Connections and the Myth of Cultural Purity* (Boston: Beacon Press, 2001), 97–125.

28. See Fiona Graham's chapter on "English Ideology" as embedded in the Oxford Union in Graham, 164–90.

29. "A team from Oxford went to the United States and debated in Massachusetts against convicts," writes Christopher Hollis in his history of the Oxford Union. See Hollis, 217. This is corroborated by Robert J. Branham in " 'I was gone on debating': Malcolm X's Prison Debates and Public Confrontations," *Argumentation and Advocacy*, Vol. 31, No. 3, Winter 1995, 117–37.

30. Jeffrey B. Perry, *Hubert Harrison: The Voice of Harlem Radicalism, 1883–1918* (New York: Columbia University Press, 2009), 7.

31. Jonathan Gill, *Harlem: The Four Hundred Year History from Dutch Village to Capital of Black America* (New York: Grove Press, 2011), 208–9.

32. "No Longer Majority Black, Harlem Is in Transition," *New York Times*, January 5, 2010.

33. "Oxford Landladies in Coloured Students Row," *Cherwell*, April 28, 1965.

34. Oxford City Council statistics: http://www.oxford.gov.uk/PageRender/decC/Population_statistics_occw.htm.

35. Roy Wilkins, Letter to Charles Longbottom, June 2, 1965, National Archives.

36. "M.P.'s visit to North America, June 1965," J. C. Edmonds, June 10, 1965, and April 15, 1965, letter re: Foley, Telegram No. 953 of April 12, National Archives.

37. Mary L. Dudziak, *Cold War Civil Rights: Race and the Image of American Democracy* (Princeton: Princeton University Press, 2002), 6.

38. Kathleen Paul, *Whitewashing Britain: Race and Citizenship in the Postwar Era* (Ithaca: Cornell University Press, 1997), 162.

39. "Margaret Thatcher Complained about Asian Immigration to Britain," *The Telegraph*, March 18, 2011. See also http://www.margaretthatcher.org/document/103485, retrieved July 25, 2013.

40. "Shoes Must not be 'Nigger' Brown," *The Times*, January 28, 1966.

41. Paul Rich, *Race and Empire in British Politics* (Cambridge: Cambridge University Press, 1990), 11

42. Catherine Hall, Keith McClelland, and Jane Rendall, *Defining the Victorian Nation: Class, Race, Gender and the Reform Act of 1867* (Cambridge: Cambridge University Press, 2000), 188–92.

43. See Paul Gilroy's discussion of the election poster in *There Ain't No Black in the Union Jack: The Cultural Politics of Race and Nation* (Chicago: University of Chicago Press, 1987), 57–58.

44. Author's conversation with David Butler, March 10, 2011, Nuffield College, Oxford University.

45. David Butler and Anthony King, *The British General Election of 1964* (London: Macmillan, 1965), 360. This is cited from Appendix III, written by Archie Singham.

46. Ibid., 361.

47. Ibid., 364.

48. Ibid., 362.

49. Malcolm X, *Malcolm X Talks to Young People: Speeches in the United States, Britain, and Africa*, ed. Steve Clark (New York: Pathfinder, 2010), 42.

50. See, for example, Edward Margolies and Michel Fabre, *The Several Lives of Chester Himes* (Jackson: University Press of Mississippi, 1997), 120.

51. Tyler Stovall, *Paris Noir: African Americans in the City of Light* (Boston: Houghton Mifflin Company, 1996), 266.

52. Malcolm seemed particularly struck by the "beautiful, slender, soft-voiced Julia." Malcolm X, with the assistance of Alex Haley, *The Autobiography of Malcolm X* (New York: Ballantine Books, 1999), 361.

53. Carlos Moore, *Pichón: A Memoir: Race and Revolution in Castro's Cuba* (Chicago: Lawrence Hill Books, 2008), 279.

54. Carew, 50.

55. Chester Himes, *My Life of Absurdity: The Autobiography of Chester Himes* (New York: Thunder's Mouth Press, 1976), 291–92.

56. Himes's memory is somewhat spotty in his account of the Paris talk, putting it closer to Malcolm's assassination than it really was. Ibid., 292.

57. Stovall, 264–68.

58. David Nicol, "Alioune Diop and the African Renaissance," *African Affairs*, Vol. 78, No. 310, January 1979, 3–11.

59. Gary P. Freeman, *Immigrant Labor and Racial Conflict in Industrial Societies: The French and British Experience, 1945–1975* (Princeton: Princeton University Press, 1979), 22–23 (tables 1 and 2).

60. The author wishes to thank Monique Wells of Entrée to Black Paris for her insights into this often overlooked community in Paris.

61. "French Minority Advocates Call for Statistics on Diversity," *France 24*, July 28, 2011. http://www.france24.com/en/20110724-france-minority-leaders-advocate-statistics-ethnic-diversity-discrimination-aneld, retrieved July 25, 2013.

62. Marable, 386.

63. "Malcolm X a la Mutualite," *Le Monde*, November 25, 1964.

64. "Paris Meeting Hears Malcolm X," *The Militant*, December 7, 1964.

65. Ibid.

66. Malcolm X, "The Black Struggle in the United States," *Presence Africaine*, English edition, No. 54, 1965, 13.

67. "Malcolm X a la Mutualité," *Le Monde*, November 25, 1964.

68. Ibid., 16.

69. Ibid., 9–10.

70. Ibid., 14–15.

71. "Paris Meeting Hears Malcolm X," *The Militant*, December 7, 1964.

72. Malcolm X, "The Black Struggle in the United States," 20.

73. Stovall, 267.

74. Himes, 292.

75. The author wishes to thank the late Manning Marable for his encouragement in placing the Oxford speech in the context of Malcolm's emergent worldview. Conversation with Professor Marable, Columbia University, New York, December 13, 2010.

76. George Breitman, ed., *Malcolm X Speaks: Selected Speeches and Statements* (New York: Grove Press, 1990), 26.

77. Ibid., 16.

78. Ali, 104.

79. Thought Equity Motion/BBC broadcast.

Chapter 2

1. Lebert Bethune recounts Malcolm's conversation with him in *Malcolm X: The Man and His Times*, ed. John Henrik Clarke (Trenton: Africa World Press, 1990), 233.

2. Malcolm X, *Malcolm X Talks to Young People: Speeches in the United States, Britain, and Africa*, ed. Steve Clark (New York: Pathfinder, 2002), 36.

3. Ibid.

4. Ibid.

5. Ibid.

6. James A. Snead, "On Repetition in Black Culture," *Black American Literature Forum*, Vol. 15, No. 4, Winter 1981, 151.

7. Jan Carew, *Ghosts in Our Blood: With Malcolm X in Africa, England, and the Caribbean* (Chicago: Lawrence Hill Books, 1994), 74.

8. The BBC hosts that evening were Ian Trethowan and Robert McKenzie. Thought Equity Motion/BBC, BBC broadcast, December 3, 1964.

9. See Manning Marable, *Malcolm X: A Life of Reinvention* (New York: Viking Press, 2011), 268.

10. Ibid., 212.

11. Alex Haley, "The Playboy Interview: Malcolm X," *Playboy*, May 1962.

12. Malcom X, *Malcolm X Talks to Young People*, 42.

13. "Malcolm Scores U.S. and Kennedy," *New York Times*, December 2, 1963.

14. Theodore White, *The Making of the President: 1964* (New York: Harper Perennial, 2010), 98.

15. Ronald Reagan, *The Reagan Diaries*, ed. Douglas Brinkley (New York: HarperCollins, 2007), 231.

16. *Malcolm X Speaks: Selected Speeches and Statements*, ed. George Breitman (New York: Grove Press, 1965), 12.

17. Barry Goldwater, *Where I Stand* (New York: McGraw-Hill, 1964), 9–16.

18. See Joseph Lowndes's account of the convention in his *From the New Deal to the New Right: Race and the Southern Origins of Modern Conservatism* (New Haven: Yale University Press, 2008), 72.

19. Barry Goldwater, *With No Apologies: The Personal and Political Memoirs of United States Senator Barry M. Goldwater* (New York: William Morrow and Company, 1979), 190.

20. The conservative political theorist Harry Jaffa provided Goldwater with the line. Its connection to Cicero and his oration against Catiline may well be only apocryphal. Ibid., 179, and 190.

21. Malcolm X with the assistance of Alex Haley, *The Autobiography of Malcolm X* (New York: Ballantine Books, 1965), 381.

22. See Daniel J. Galvin on "Operation Dixie" and Republican party-building efforts in the South in *Presidential Party Building: Dwight D. Eisenhower to George W. Bush* (Princeton: Princeton University Press, 2010), 63–67. Goldwater swept the Deep South in 1964, taking South Carolina, Georgia, Alabama, Mississippi, and Louisiana. Along with his home state of Arizona, these were his only electoral victories.

23. Malcolm X, *Malcolm X Talks to Young People*, 47.

24. "Goldwater—the Great American Dreamer," *Isis*, week ending November 7, 1964.

25. "What's the Mainstream? Who Is in It?" *New York Times*, September 6, 1964.

26. "Wilkins Says Goldwater Victory Might Bring about Police State," *New York Times*, September 7, 1964.

27. Malcolm X, *Malcolm X Talks to Young People*, 37–38.

28. John Locke, *The Two Treatises of Government and a Letter Concerning Toleration* (Stillwell, KS: Digireads.com, 2005), 123.

29. Malcolm X, *Malcolm X Talks to Young People*, 38.

30. Ibid.

31. See Fanon's *Black Skin, White Masks* (1951), trans. Charles Lam Markman (New York: Grove Press, 1967), and *The Wretched of the Earth* (1961), trans. Constance Farrington (New York: Grove Press, 1963).

32. Malcolm X, *By Any Means Necessary* (New York: Pathfinder, 1992), 149–50.

33. Ibid., 153.

34. Alvin Tillery Jr., *Between Homeland and Motherland: Africa, U.S. Foreign Policy, and Black Leadership in America* (Ithaca: Cornell University Press, 2011), 118.

35. Letter from British Embassy, Moscow, June 13, 1963 (FO 135/13/6), National Archives, London (hereafter National Archives).

36. Malcolm X, *Malcolm X Talks to Young People*, 39.

37. Ibid., 37.

38. Letter from Robert Owen to S. J. Aspden, British Embassy, Washington, DC, March 26, 1965 (J10314 5/9), National Archives; emphasis added.

39. Malcolm is quoted in Mary L. Dudziak, *Cold War Civil Rights: Race and the Image of American Democracy* (Princeton: Princeton University Press, 2000), 222.

40. "Mr. Griffiths Faces the Immigrants," *The Guardian*, October 13, 1964.

41. Author's conversation with David Butler, March 10, 2011, Nuffield College, Oxford University.

42. "Malcolm X Off to Smethwick," *Times of London*, February 12, 1965.

43. Harold Macmillan, *At the End of the Day: 1961–63* (New York: Harper and Row, 1973), 73.

44. Kathleen Paul, *Whitewashing Britain: Race and Citizenship in the Postwar Era* (Ithaca: Cornell University, 1997), 163.

45. "Immigration Problems," *The Guardian*, August 8, 1962.

46. Teresa Hayter, *The Case Against Immigration Controls* (Ann Arbor: Pluto Press, 2004), 45.

47. "Tories Use Race Issues, Says Vicar," *The Observer*, September 27, 1964.

48. "BBC Cancels Smethwick Report," *The Guardian*, September 18, 1964.

49. "Smethwick Not to Hear Mr. Powell," *The Guardian*, September 24, 1964.

50. "Rebuff for Tory at Smethwick," *The Observer*, October 4, 1964.

51. "Tories Disown Anti-Negro Posters," *The Guardian*, October 8, 1964.

52. Malcolm X, *Malcolm X Talks to Young People*, 42.

53. Paul, 178.

54. Malcolm X, *Malcolm X Speaks*, 26.

55. Malcolm X, *Malcolm X Talks to Young People*, 42.

56. Thought Equity Motion/BBC broadcast.

57. Diary entries, the Malcolm X Collection: Papers (1948–1965), Box 9, Notebook 8, Schomberg Center for Research in Black Culture, New York Public Library.

58. Malcolm X, *Malcolm X Talks to Young People*, 45.

59. See the OED online: http://www.oed.com/view/Entry/157084?redirect edFrom=racialism#.

60. Kwame Anthony Appiah, *In My Father's House: Africa in the Philosophy of Culture* (Oxford: Oxford University Press, 1992), 13. Appiah makes the case that W. E. B. Du Bois was a racialist in this sense. Perhaps the best "folk" theory of racialism was offered by the late American football player, the Reverend Reggie White, who once argued that such racial traits were "gifts" from God. See "Remarks by Packers' White Draw Criticism," *New York Times*, March 26, 1998.

61. Perhaps the earliest example to appear in book form was Sir John Willison's chapter "Imperialism and Racialism," in *Sir Wilfred Laurier and the Liberal Party: A Political History* (Toronto: George N. Morang and Company, 1903).

62. The use of the word may be charted courtesy of Google's "Books Ngram Viewer." I wish to thank my colleague at Lehigh University, Holona Ochs, for her assistance with this research tool.

63. Malcolm X, *Malcolm X Talks to Young People*, 39.

64. See Keith D. Miller's "Plymouth Rock Landed on Us: Malcolm X's Whiteness Theory as a Basis for Alternative Literacy," *College Composition and Communication*, Vol. 56, No. 2, December 2004, 199–222.

65. Malcolm X, *Malcolm X Talks to Young People*, 39.

66. Ibid., 47.

67. Ibid., 41.

68. Ibid., 43.

69. Ibid.

70. "Gallery on BBC-1," *The Guardian*, December 4, 1964. Italics added for emphasis.

Chapter 3

1. Malcolm X Collection: Papers (1948–1965) (hereafter Malcolm X Papers), SC Micro R 6270, Box 13, Folder 2, Reel 13, Schomburg Center for Research in Black Cuture, New York Public Library.

2. James H. Cone, *Martin and Malcolm and America: A Dream or a Nightmare* (Maryknoll: Orbis Books, 1991), 118.

3. Manning Marable, *Malcolm X: A Life of Reinvention* (New York: Viking, 2011), 229.

4. James Farmer, *Lay Bare the Heart: An Autobiography of the Civil Rights Movement* (New York: Arbor House, 1998), 227–30.

5. Malcolm X, Letter to Maya Angelou c/o Julian Mayfield, January 15, 1965, Malcolm X Papers, SC Micro R 6270, Box 4, Folder 5, Reel 4. David Du Bois was the stepson of W. E. B. Du Bois.

6. Mary L. Dudziak, *Cold War Civil Rights: Race and the Image of American Democracy* (Princeton: Princeton University Press, 2000), 226.

7. Malcolm X Papers, SC Micro R 6270, Box 13, Folder 2, Reel 13.

8. Malcolm X, *Malcolm X Talks to Young People: Speeches in the United States, Britain, and Africa* (New York: Pathfinder, 2002), 37, 45. For audio of the address see http://filepedia.org/audio/the-oxford-union-debate-1964.

9. Malcolm X with the assistance of Alex Haley, *The Autobiography of Malcolm X* (New York: Ballantine Books, 1991), 209.

10. Marable, 290.

11. "I said to myself he is choosing martyrdom," recalled Jan Carew of Malcolm's refusal to go into exile. Jan Carew, *Ghosts in Our Blood: With Malcolm X in Africa, England, and the Caribbean* (Chicago: Lawrence Hill Books: 1994), 58–59.

12. Malcolm X Papers, SC Micro R 6270, Box 9, Diaries, Notebook 3.

13. Ibid.

14. Letter from Sandra M. Devoto to Malcolm X, December 5, 1964, Malcolm X Papers, SC Micro R 6270, Box 4, General Correspondence, Folder 5, Reel 4.

15. Malcolm X, *The Autobiography of Malcolm X*, 292.

16. Marable, 135.

17. C. Eric Lincoln, *The Black Muslims in America* (Grand Rapids: Wm. Eerdmans Publishing, 1994), 71.

18. Peter L. Goldman, *The Death and Life of Malcolm X* (New York: Illini Books, 1979), 135.

19. Excerpted from Arnold Perl's 1972 documentary *Malcolm X* (Warner Bros.) http://www.youtube.com/watch?v=lx7RecMy2og&feature=related.

20. *Tonight* broadcast, BBC, November 20, 1964; courtesy of Thought Equity Motion.

21. "Paul R. Reynolds, literary agent for many top writers, dies," *New York Times,* June 11, 1988.

22. Malcolm X letter to Mr. Paul R. Reynolds, March 21, 1964, Malcolm X Papers, SC Micro R 6270, Box 4, Folder 5, Reel 4.

23. Letter from 153 Lenox Avenue to Mr. Malcolm Little, August 15, 1964, Malcolm X Papers, SC Micro R 6270, Box 4, Folder 5, Reel 4.

24. Michael Eric Dyson, *Making Malcolm: The Myth and Meaning of Malcolm X* (Oxford: Oxford University Press, 1995).

25. Richard S. Newman, *Freedom's Prophet: Bishop Richard Allen, the AME Church, and the Black Founding Fathers* (New York: New York University Press, 2008), 45.

26. Nell Irvin Painter, *Sojourner Truth: A Life, A Symbol* (New York: W. W. Norton, 1996), 74–75.

27. Newman, 45.

28. Edward J. Blum, *W.E.B. Du Bois: American Prophet* (Philadelphia: University of Pennsylvania Press, 2007), 60.

29. Malcolm X, *Malcolm X Talks to Young People*, 37–38.

30. Carew, 103.

31. Ibid., 46.

32. Ibid., 49.

33. Ibid., 45.

34. Thought Equity Motion/BBC, BBC broadcast, December 3, 1964. (first mention this chapter).

35. Hugh MacDiarmid, *The Company I've Kept: Essays in Autobiography* (Berkeley: University of California Press, 1967), 27.

36. Carew, 45.

37. Goldman, 11.

38. Malcolm X, *Malcolm X Talks to Young People*, 41.

39. Malcolm X Papers, SC Micro R 6270, Box 13, Folder 2, Reel 13.

40. Walter MacDougal, *Freedom Just around the Corner: A New American History, 1585–1828* (New York: Harper Perennial, 2005), 155.

41. Malcolm X, *Malcolm X Speaks: Selected Speeches and Statements*, ed. George Breitman (New York: Grove Press, 1965, 158–59.

42. Ibid., 161.

43. Joe Street, "Malcolm X, Smethwick, and the Influence of the African American Freedom Struggle on British Race Relations in the 1960s," *Journal of Black Studies*, Vol. 38, No. 6, 2008, 935.

44. "Cameron Criticizes 'Multiculturalism' in Britain," *New York Times*, February 5, 2011.

45. Mike Phillips and Trevor Phillips, *Windrush: The Irresistible Rise of Multi-Racial Britain* (London: HarperCollins, 1998), 1–4.

46. Stephen Tuck, *We Ain't What We Ought to Be: The Black Freedom Struggle from Emancipation to Obama* (Cambridge: Harvard University Press, 2010), 280.

47. Street, 932–34.

48. Mr. Dennis Greenhill message dated March 16, 1965, National Archives, Foreign Office files.

49. President Lyndon B. Johnson telegram to Prime Minister Harold Wilson, March 24, 1965, National Archives, Foreign Office files.

50. Paul Foot, *Immigration and Race in British Politics* (Middlesex: Penguin, 1965), 250.

51. Malcolm X, *Malcolm X Talks to Young People*, 37, 49.

52. *Tonight* broadcast, BBC, November 20, 1964; courtesy of Thought Equity Motion.

53. Mike Wallace, *Between You and Me: A Memoir* (New York: Hyperion, 2005), 88.

54. Abraham Lincoln, *Complete Works*, ed. John Nicolay and John Hay (New York: The Century Co., 1894), 513.

55. Malcolm X, *Malcolm X Talks to Young People*, 38.

56. Ibid., 49.

57. Malcolm X, *Malcolm X Speaks*, 8.

58. Martin Luther King Jr., *A Testament of Hope: The Essential Writings and Speeches of Martin Luther King, Jr.*, ed. James M. Washington (New York: HarperCollins, 1986), 233.

59. Author's interview with Shirley Anderson Fletcher, June 19, 2012.

60. Ibid.

61. Carew, 94.

62. http://www.youtube.com/watch?v=f2S3ShBexMs.

Chapter 4

1. This had been Manning Marable and a number of scholars' chief critiques of Alex Haley's *Autobiography*. See, for example, "The Missing Malcolm: An

Interview with Manning Marable," *International Socialist Review*, Issue 63, January–February 2009, http://www.isreview.org/issues/63/feat-malcolmx.shtml.

2. Graeme Abernethy, " 'Not Just an American Problem': Malcolm X in Britain," *Atlantic Studies*, Vol. 7, No. 3, September 2010, 297.

3. Thomas Frank, *The Conquest of Cool: Business Culture, Counterculture, and the Rise of Hip Consumerism* (Chicago: University of Chicago Press, 1998).

4. http://www.esquire.com/the-side/style-guides/celebrity-sunglasses-for-men-malcolm-x#slide-5.

5. The full audio portion of the debate, including Berkeley's speech, can be found at http://www.brothermalcolm.net/2003/mx_oxford/index.html.

6. "Malcolm X Postal Stamp Makes Debut," *Los Angeles Times*, January 28, 1999.

7. "What He Might Have Become," *The Economist*, April 7, 2011. The correction was published in the April 14, 2011, print edition.

8. For his part, Hugh MacDiarmid was described by Berkeley as "an apostle of economic absolutism." http://www.brothermalcolm.net/2003/mx_oxford/index.html.

9. http://www.brothermalcolm.net/2003/mx_oxford/index.html.

10. Ibid.

11. Travel notebook, Thursday, September 24, 1964, 1964, the Malcolm X Collection: Papers (1948–1965) (hereafter Malcolm X Papers), Schomburg Center for Research in Black Culture, New York Public Library.

12. "Malcolm X Stirs Concern of U.S.," *New York Times*, August 13, 1964.

13. Thought Equity Motion/BBC, BBC broadcast, December 3, 1964.

14. "The Night Malcolm X Came to Brown," *Brown Alumni Magazine*, April 2012.

15. For Malcolm's response to Kissinger, see Marilyn X, Letter to Henry Kissinger (undated, re: June 5, 1964 Kissinger letter), Malcolm X Papers, Box 3, Speaking Engagements. For John Kerry's letter see John F. Kerry, letter to Mr. Malcolm X, August 15, 1964, Malcolm X Papers, Box 3, Speaking Engagements.

16. Malcolm says "1984" for what, presumably, should be "1894," as he walks the audience back in time in increments of thirty years. Malcolm X, *Malcolm X Talks to Young People: Speeches in the United States, Britain, and Africa*, ed. Steve Clark (New York: Pathfinder, 2002), 46.

17. Ibid., 67–69.

18. Alexis de Tocqueville, *Democracy in America*, ed. Harvey Mansfield and Debra Winthrop (Chicago: University of Chicago Press, 2000), 343.

19. Malcolm X, *Malcolm X Talks to Young People*, 46; emphasis added.

20. Ibid., 49.

21. Daniel J. Galvin, *Presidential Party Building: Dwight D. Eisenhower to George W. Bush* (Princeton: Princeton University Press, 2010), 63–67.

22. Robert A. Caro, *The Passage of Power: The Years of Lyndon B. Johnson* (New York: Alfred A. Knopf, 2012), 109–44.

23. "Moderates in G.O.P. Challenge Goldwater Control of Party," *New York Times*, November 5, 1964.

24. Rick Perlstein, *Nixonland: The Rise of a President and the Fracturing of America* (New York: Scribner, 2008), 79–80.

25. "300 Negroes Riot in Philadelphia," *New York Times*, August 29, 1964.

26. Malcolm X, *Malcolm X Talks to Young People*, 56.

27. Letter to Mr. Mayhew from British Embassy, August 18, 1965, Confidential Ref: 1016, National Archives, London (hereafter National Archives).

28. Foreign Office, Telegram (from Mr. Wilford, Peking) No. 1018, August 19, 1965, National Archives.

29. Brian Harrison, ed., *The History of the University of Oxford*, Vol. 8: *The Twentieth Century* (Oxford: Oxford University Press, 1994), 53.

30. Ibid., 723.

31. Joseph A. Soares, *The Decline of Privilege: The Modernization of Oxford University* (Stanford: Stanford University Press, 1999), 36.

32. University of Oxford, Undergraduate Admissions Statistics: Ethnic Origin, 2011. Harvard and Princeton Universities, by way of example, are far more diverse in this regard, that is, with respect to race. http://www.ox.ac.uk/about_the_university/facts_and_figures/undergraduate_admissions_statistics/ethnic_origin.html.

33. Plowden Report, written by Burke Trend, January 31, 1964, CAB 129/116, National Archives.

34. Malcolm X, *Malcolm X Talks to Young People*, 38.

35. Plowden Report, written by Burke Trend, January 31, 1964, CAB 129/116, National Archives.

36. "Enoch Powell's 'Rivers of Blood' Speech," *Telegraph*, November 6, 2007.

37. John Dumbrell, *A Special Relationship: Anglo American Relations from the Cold War to Iraq* (New York: Palgrave Macmillan, 2006), 35.

38. The text of Powell's speech can be found, among many places, on the website of the *Daily Telegraph*: http://www.telegraph.co.uk/comment/3643823/Enoch-Powells-Rivers-of-Blood-speech.html.

39. The 1793 letter to James Monroe can be found in Ashli White's *Encountering Revolution: Haiti and the Making of the Early Republic* (Baltimore: Johns Hopkins University Press, 2010), 1–2.

40. Enoch Powell, *No Easy Answers* (New York: Seabury Press, 1973), 105–7.

41. "Churchill Grandson Urges Halt to Flow of Immigrants," *Los Angeles Times*, May 30, 1993.

42. "Sarah Kennedy 'Spoken to' by BBC for Praising Enoch Powell during Radio 2 Show," *Mail Online*, July 19, 2009. See http://www.dailymail.co.uk/news/article-1200523/Sarah-Kennedy-reprimanded-BBC-praising-Enoch-Powell-Radio-2-show.html#ixzz1xhJQaifH.

43. "Millions of Britons See Malcolm X in TV Broadcast of Debate at Oxford," *The Militant*, December 4, 1964.

44. Jeff Walden of the BBC's Written Archives provided these figures. The broadcast produced a "Reaction Index" of 68, well above average for a program of this nature and time. Author's conversation with Mr. Walden, May 23, 2012.

45. Max Weber, among others, has been enlisted in making this argument. See commentary and notes in Mustafa Akyol's *Islam without Extremes: A Muslim Case for Liberty* (New York: W. W. Norton, 2011), 76, 298.

46. See Manning Marable on Malcolm's nascent relationship with Che Guevara. Marable suggests that Malcolm and Guevara may have met roughly one week after Oxford. Manning Marable, *Malcolm X: A Life of Reinvention* (New York: Viking, 2011), 394–96.

47. Ibid., 198. Franz Fanon also was struck by Hegel's master-slave dialectic. Marable notes, 523.

48. Thought Equity Motion/BBC broadcast.

49. The umrah involves a series of optional religious rituals performed in Mecca. Unlike the hajj, it may be undertaken any time during the year.

50. Malcolm X Collection, Schomburg Center for Research in Black Culture.

51. Akyol, 90–93.

52. Author's telephone interview with Tariq Ali, May 22, 2012.

53. Thought Equity Motion/BBC broadcast.

54. Ibid.

55. Ibid.

56. The remark could not be picked up by the BBC broadcast, but it was confirmed to the author by Christie Davies. Author's telephone interview with Mr. Davies, June 11, 2012.

57. Thought Equity Motion/BBC broadcast.

58. Ibid.

59. Ibid.

60. Author's telephone interview with Christie Davies, June 11, 2012.

61. "Malcolm X," *Beaver*, March 4, 1965.

62. Graeme Abernethy, " 'Not Just an American Problem': Malcolm X in Britain," *Atlantic Studies*, Vol. 7, No. 3, September 2010, 291–94.

63. Mike Phillips and Trevor Phillips, *Windrush: The Irresistible Rise of Multi-Racial Britain* (London: HarperCollins, 1998), 240.

64. Ibid., 236.

65. Author's telephone interview with Tariq Ali, May 22, 2012.

66. Author's telephone interview with Christie Davies, June 11, 2012.

67. Phillips and Phillips, 241.

68. Author's telephone interview with Shirley Fletcher, June 19, 2012.

Chapter 5

1. Malcolm X, *Malcolm X Talks to Young People: Speeches in the United States, Britain, and Africa* (New York: Pathfinder, 2010), 50.

2. Albert Camus, *The Rebel: An Essay on Man in Revolt*, trans. Anthony Bower (New York: Vintage Books, 1956), 13.

3. Anthony Sampson, *Mandela: The Authorized Biography* (London: Vintage, 2000), 230–32.

4. Robert J. Branham, " 'I was gone on debating': Malcolm X's Prison Debates and Public Confrontations," *Argumentation and Advocacy*, Vol. 31, No. 3, Winter 1995, 117–37.

5. Malcolm X, *Malcolm X Talks to Young People*, 50.

6. Simon Malley, "Who Killed Malcolm X?" *Jeune Afrique*, March 7, 1965.

7. Robert E. Terrill, ed., *The Cambridge Companion to Malcolm X* (Cambridge: Cambridge University Press, 2010) 135.

8. Malcolm X, *Malcolm X Talks to Young People*, 119–20.

9. Louis A. De Caro Jr., *On the Side of My People: A Religious Life of Malcolm X* (New York: New York University Press, 1996), 248.

10. "Obama's Oslo Remarks," *New York Times*, December 10, 2009.

11. http://www.youtube.com/watch?feature=player_detailpage&v=i4VTPQ K0apY.

12. Malcolm X, *Malcolm X Speaks: Selected Speeches and Statements*, ed. George Breitman (New York: Grove Press, 1965), 12.

13. Ibid., 33.

14. Mustafa Akyol, *Islam without Extremes: A Muslim Case for Liberty* (New York: W. W. Norton, 2011), 52–53.

15. Diary entry, May 11, 1964, the Malcolm X Collection: Papers (1948–1965) (hereafter Malcolm X Papers), Box 9, Diaries, Notebook 6, Schomburg Center for Research in Black Culture, New York Public Library.

16. See E. E. Schattschneider's *The Semisovereign People: A Realist's View of Democracy in America* (New York: Wadsworth Publishing, 1975).

17. Malcolm does not jump to the latter conclusion initially in his diary, but he does raise the possibility of an attempt upon his life weeks later. Manning Marable, *Malcolm X: A Life of Reinvention* (New York: Viking, 2011), 364.

18. Malcolm X Papers, Box 9, Diaries, Notebook 6.

19. Diary entry, April 26, 1964, Malcolm X Papers, Box 9, Diaries, Notebook 6.

20. Diary entry, September 23, 1964, Malcolm X Papers, Box 9, Diaries, Notebook 6.

21. Michael Hardt and Antonio Negri, *Commonwealth* (Cambridge: Harvard University Press, 2011), 336.

22. Ibid., 326.

23. http://www.youtube.com/watch?v=ZUVzyvWUsjQ.

24. Diary entry, May 11, 1964, Malcolm X Papers, Box 9, Diaries, Notebook 6.

25. http://www.washingtonpost.com/politics/decision2012/2012-presidential-debate-president-obama-and-mitt-romneys-remarks-at-lynn-university-on-oct-22-running-transcript/2012/10/22/be8899d6-1c7a-11e2-9cd5-b55c38388962_story.html.

26. The Bureau of Investigative Journalism estimates the total number of civilian deaths caused by US drone strikes may be greater than the number of civilians killed during the September 11 attacks on the United States in 2001. http://www.thebureauinvestigates.com/2012/10/15/counting-the-bodies-in-the-pakistani-drone-campaign/.

27. Malcolm X, *Malcolm X Talks to Young People*, 39.

28. Malcolm X, Malcolm X Speaks, 197–98.

29. See the chapter "The Merchant Is Always a Stranger," in Vijay Prashad, *Everybody Was Kung Fu Fighting: Afro-Asian Connections and the Myth of Cultural Purity* (Boston: Beacon Press, 2001), 104–11.

30. Yuri Kochiyama, "The Impact of Malcolm X on Asian-American Politics and Activism," in *Blacks, Latinos, and Asians in Urban America: Status and Prospects for Politics and Activism*, ed. James Jennings (London: Praeger, 1994), 132–33.

31. Author's telephone interview with Shirley Anderson Fletcher, June 19, 2012.

32. United States Government Memorandum, Director, FBI, 100-441765, December 8, 1964. The document can be found at the Malcolm X Project at Columbia University. http://www.columbia.edu/cu/ccbh/mxp/pdf/chinenukes.pdf.

33. Tim Weiner, *Enemies: A History of the FBI* (New York: Random House, 2012), 199 n. 483.

34. Author's interview with Shirley Anderson Fletcher, June 19, 2012.

35. Author's interview with Carlos Moore, June 13, 2012.

36. Manning Marable's biography addressed the uncertainties of the assassination directly, implicating the New York Police Department and FBI as enabling, if not directly participating in, the assassination. See Marable, 450–78.

37. March 8, 1965, FBI file 106-399321. The document can be found at the Malcolm X Project at Columbia University. http://www.columbia.edu/cu/ccbh/mxp/govdocs.html.

38. "The Death of Malcolm X," filed by Richard E. Webb, February 23, 1965, Foreign Office, National Archives, London.

39. Ibid.

40. "Black Brotherhood," *Beaver*, February 18, 1965.

41. "Malcolm X," *Beaver*, March 4, 1965.

42. "James Baldwin: At the Union," *Isis*, March 6, 1965.

43. Ibid.

44. "Baldwin Blames White 'Climate,'" *Los Angeles Times*, February 22, 1965.

45. "After Malcolm X," *Times*, February 23, 1965.

46. "Malcolm X Shot Dead at Harlem Rally," *Times*, February 22, 1965.

47. "Malcolm X, the Apostle of Violence," *Guardian*, February 22, 1965.

48. "After Malcolm X," *Times*, February 23, 1965.

49. "Le leader nationaliste Malcolm X est assassin par un commando de Noirs," *Le Monde*, February 23, 1965.

50. *L'Humanité* covered the assassination on its front page as well, via a photograph of Malcolm being carried off to the hospital surrounded by policemen. "Malcolm X se preparait a denouncer la collusion entre les "black muslims" et certain millieux reactionnaires," *L'Humanité*, February 23, 1965.

51. Ibid.

52. "L'Heritage de Malcolm X," *La Vie Africaine*, No. 57, April 1965.

53. Diary entry, June 16, 1964(?), Malcolm X Papers, Box 9, Diaries, Notebook 6.

54. Diary entry, Malcolm X Papers, Box 9, Diaries, Notebook 8.

55. Author's interview with Tim Gopsill, November 6, 2012.

56. Conversation with author, March 2011.

57. Conversation with author, March 2011.

58. Conversation with author, October 27, 2011.

59. Conversation with author, March, 2011.

Chapter 6

1. Author's telephone interview with Tariq Ali, May 22, 2012.

2. Ibid.

3. Oxford Union Library records.

4. Author's telephone interview with Christie Davies, June 11, 2012.

5. Ibid.

6. Paul Gilroy, *After Empire: Melancholia or Convivial Culture?* (Abingdon: Routledge, 2010).

7. Jan Carew, *Ghosts in Our Blood: With Malcolm X in Africa, England, and the Caribbean* (Chicago: Lawrence Hill Books, 1994), 72–73.

8. Author's telephone interview with Tariq Ali, May 22, 2012.

9. Ibid.

10. "Anthony Abrahams, Dead at 71," *Jamaica Observer*, August 8, 2012. http://www.jamaicaobserver.com/news/Anthony-Abrahams--dead-at-71_9396201.

11. Author's interview with Richard D. Fletcher, June 18, 2012.

12. Shirley F. Anderson, *The Dance of Difference: The New Frontier of Sexual Orientation* (Bethesda, MD: Pearson, 2010).

13. Author's interview with Shirley Anderson Fletcher, June 18, 2012.

14. Ibid.

15. Manning Marable, *Malcolm X: A Life of Reinvention* (New York: Viking, 2011), 390, 391.

16. Author's telephone interview with Tariq Ali, May 22, 2012.

17. Author's interview with Shirley Anderson Fletcher, June 18, 2012.

18. Ibid.

19. See, for example, Herb Boyd, Ron Daniels, Maulana Karenga, and Haki R. Madhubuti, eds., *By Any Means Necessary Malcolm X: Real, Not Invented* (Chicago: Third World Press, 2012). The edited volume includes a veritable who's who of Black Nationalist and intellectual thought among the contributors..

20. Author's telephone interview with Carlos Moore, Wednesday, June 13, 2012.

21. Ibid.

22. Ibid.

23. Ibid.

24. Ibid.

25. Ibid.

26. Ibid.

27. Ibid.

28. Ibid.

29. Ibid.

30. Valerie Amiraux and Patrick Simon, "There Are No Minorities Here: Cultures of Scholarship and Public Debate on Immigrants and Integration in France," *International Journal of Comparative Sociology*, Vol. 47, Nos. 3–4, August 2006, 191–215.

31. Author's interview with Pap Ndiaye, July 4, 2012.

32. Ibid.

33. Ibid.

34. Ibid.

35. Pap Ndiaye, *La Condition Noire: Essai sur une minorite francaise* (Paris: Gallimard Education, 2008), 34.

36. Carlos Moore, original unedited transcript, speech at the Maubert Mutualité, February 9, 1965, Carlos Moore Collection, Ralph J. Bunche Center for African American Studies, University of California, Los Angeles.

37. Author's interview with Pap Ndiaye, July 4, 2012.

38. Ibid.

39. http://www.youtube.com/watch?v=74_pFXwRgCE.

40. Bruno Lemesle, "La Priere a l'heure de l'Apero." Photographed in Paris, date unknown.

41. See for example, "Social Ills Feed Rise of Far-Right Party in France," *New York Times*, March 27, 2011.

42. Mary Dudziak, *Cold War Civil Rights: Race and the Image of American Democracy* (Princeton: Princeton University Press, 2000), 141.

43. "US Courts the Support of French Muslims," *New York Times*, May 26, 2008.

44. Ibid.

45. "For Blacks in France, Obama's Rise Is Reason to Rejoice, and to Hope," *New York Times*, June 17, 2008.

46. Ibid.

47. Robert S. Leiken, *Europe's Angry Muslims: The Revolt of the Second Generation* (Oxford: Oxford University Press, 2012), 37–38.

48. Ibid.

49. Author's interview with Pap Ndiaye, July 4, 2012.

50. Jim House and Neil MacMaster, *Paris 1961: Algerians, State Terror, and Memory* (Oxford: Oxford University Press, 2009), 274.

51. Malcolm X, *By Any Means Necessary* (New York: Pathfinder, 1992), 146.

52. Gilroy, 115.

53. "Plaque to Honour Malcolm X Visit to Smethwick in 1965," *BBC News*, February 21, 2012. http://www.bbc.co.uk/news/uk-england-birmingham-17102185.

54. Author's telephone interview with Christie Davies, June 11, 2012.

55. Oxford University undergraduate admission statistics. http://ox.ac.uk/about_the_university/facts_and_figures/.

56. Debate brochure, Oxford Union Society, March 24, 2012.

57. Author's telephone interview with Tariq Ali, May 22, 2012.

Epilogue

1. Author's conversation with Rev. Jesse Jackson, February 13, 2012.

BIBLIOGRAPHY

ARCHIVES

BBC Written Archives, London, UK
British National Archives, Kew, UK
Institute of Race Relations, London, UK
Oxford University Archives, Oxford, UK
Oxfordshire Record Office, Oxford, UK
Thought Equity Motion/BBC (video recordings), Denver, CO

LIBRARIES

British National Library, London
British Library of Political & Economic Science, London School of Economics
L'Institut du Monde Arabe, Paris
Ralph J. Bunche Center for African American Studies, Carlos Moore Collection, UCLA
Schomburg Center for Research in Black Culture, the Malcolm X Collection Black Culture, the Malcolm X Collection, New York Public Library
University of Oxford, Bodleian Library
University of Warwick, Sivanandan Collection

NEWSPAPERS

Amsterdam News
Cherwell (Oxford University)
Le Figaro
The Guardian
L'Humanité

Isis (Oxford University)
The Listener
The Militant
Le Monde
New York Times
The Observer
Oxford Mail
The Sun
Telegraph
The Times (London)

INTERVIEWS

Tariq Ali, May 22, 2012
Christie Davies, June 11, 2012
Shirley Anderson Fletcher, June 18, 2012
Tim Gopsill, November 6, 2012
Carlos Moore, June 13, 2012
Pap Ndiaye, July 4, 2012

ARTICLES

Graeme Abernethy, " 'Not Just an American Problem': Malcolm X in Britain," *Atlantic Studies*, Vol. 7, No. 3, 2010, 285–307.

Robert J. Branham, " 'I was gone on debating': Malcolm X's Prison Debates and Public Confrontations," *Argumentation and Advocacy*, Vol. 31, No. 3, Winter 1995, 117–37.

John Immerwahr, "Hume's Revised Racism," *Journal of the History of Ideas*, Vol. 53, No. 3, July–September 1992, 481–86.

Desmond S. King and Rogers M. Smith, "Racial Orders in American Political Development," *American Political Science Review*, Vol. 99, No. 1, February 2005, 75–92.

Malcolm X, "The Black Struggle in the United States," *Presence Africaine*, English edition, No. 54, 1965, 8–27.

James A. Snead, "On Repetition in Black Culture," *Black American Literature Forum*, Vol. 15, No. 4, Winter 1981, 146–54.

Joe Street, "Malcolm X, Smethwick, and the Influence of the African American Freedom Struggle on British Race Relations in the 1960s," *Journal of Black Studies*, Vol. 38, No. 6, 2008, 932–50.

BOOKS

Mustafa Akyol, *Islam without Extremes: A Muslim Case for Liberty*, New York: W.W. Norton, 2011.

Tariq Ali, *Street Fighting Years: An Autobiography of the Sixties*, New York: Verso, 2005.

Judy G. Batson, *Her Oxford*, Nashville: Vanderbilt University Press, 2008.

Edward J. Blum, *W.E.B. Du Bois: American Prophet*, Philadelphia: University of Pennsylvania Press, 2007.

David Butler and Anthony King, *The British General Election of 1964*, London: Macmillan and Company, 1965.

Albert Camus, *The Rebel: An Essay on Man in Revolt*, trans. Anthony Bower, New York: Vintage Books, 1956.

Jan Carew, *Ghosts in Our Blood: With Malcolm X in Africa, England, and the Caribbean*, Chicago: Lawrence Hill Books, 1994.

James H. Cone, *Martin and Malcolm and America: A Dream or a Nightmare*, Maryknoll: Orbis Books, 1991.

Gerald L. Davis, *I Got the Word in Me and I Can Sing It, You Know: A Study of the Performed African-American Sermon*, Philadelphia: University of Pennsylvania Press, 1987.

Ossie Davis, "Eulogy for Malcolm X," in *For Malcolm: Poems on the Life and the Death of Malcolm X*, ed. Dudley Randall and Margaret G. Burroughs, Detroit: Broadside Press, 1969, 122.

Mary L. Dudziak, *Cold War Civil Rights: Race and the Image of American Democracy*. Princeton: Princeton University Press, 2002.

John Dumbrell, *A Special Relationship: Anglo American Relations from the Cold War to Iraq*, New York: Palgrave Macmillan, 2006.

Michael Eric Dyson, *Making Malcolm: The Myth and Meaning of Malcolm X*, Oxford: Oxford University Press, 1995.

Frantz Fanon, *Black Skin, White Masks*, trans. Charles Lam Markmann, New York: Grove Press, 1967.

——, *The Wretched of the Earth*, trans. Constance Farrington, New York: Grove Press, 1963.

James Farmer, *Lay Bare the Heart: An Autobiography of the Civil Rights Movement*, New York: Arbor House, 1998.

Paul Foot, *Immigration and Race in British Politics*, Middlesex: Penguin, 1965.

Gary P. Freeman, *Immigrant Labor and Racial Conflict in Industrial Societies: The French and British Experience 1945–1975*, Princeton: Princeton University Press, 1979.

Jonathan Gill, *Harlem: The Four Hundred Year History from Dutch Village to Capital of Black America*, New York: Grove Press, 2011.

———. *After Empire: Melancholia or Convivial Culture?* London: Routledge, 2004.

Paul Gilroy, *There Ain't No Black in the Union Jack: The Cultural Politics of Race and Nation*. Chicago: University of Chicago Press, 1987.

Peter L. Goldman, *The Death and Life of Malcolm X*, New York: Illini Books, 1979.

Fiona Graham, *Playing at Politics: Ethnography of the Oxford Union*, Edinburgh: Dunedin Academic Press, 2005.

Catherine Hall, Keith McClelland, and Jane Rendall, *Defining the Victorian Nation: Class, Race, Gender and the Reform Act of 1867*, Cambridge: Cambridge University Press, 2000.

Brian Harrison, ed., *The History of the University of Oxford*, Vol. 8: *The Twentieth Century*, Oxford: Oxford University Press, 1994.

Chester Himes, *My Life of Absurdity: The Autobiography of Chester Himes*, New York: Thunder's Mouth Press, 1976.

Christopher Hollis, *The Oxford Union*, London: Evans Brothers Limited, 1965.

Jim House and Neil MacMaster, *Paris 1961: Algerians, State Terror, and Memory*, Oxford: Oxford University Press, 2009.

Martin Luther King Jr., *A Testament of Hope: The Essential Writings and Speeches of Martin Luther King, Jr.*, ed. James M. Washington, New York: HarperCollins, 1986.

Yuri Kochiyama, "The Impact of Malcolm X on Asian-American Politics and Activism," in *Blacks, Latinos, and Asians in Urban America: Status and Prospects for Politics and Activism*, ed. James Jennings, London: Praeger, 1994, 129–42.

Robert S. Leiken, *Europe's Angry Muslims: The Revolt of the Second Generation*, Oxford: Oxford University Press, 2012.

Abraham Lincoln, *Abraham Lincoln: Complete Works*, ed. John Nicolay and John Hay, New York: The Century Co., 1894.

C. Eric Lincoln, *The Black Muslims in America*, Grand Rapids: Wm. Eerdmans Publishing, 1994.

Hugh MacDiarmid, *The Company I've Kept: Essays in Autobiography*, Berkeley: University of California Press, 1967.

Malcolm X, *Autobiography of Malcolm X*, New York: Ballantine Books, 1999.

———, *By Any Means Necessary: Malcolm X*, New York: Pathfinder, 1992.

———, *Malcolm X Speaks: Selected Speeches and Statements*, ed. George Breitman, New York: Grove Press, 1965.

———, *Malcolm X Talks to Young People*, ed. Steve Clark, New York: Pathfinder Press, 2002.

John Stuart Mill, "The Negro Question 1850," in *The Collected Works of John Stuart Mill*, Vol. 21: *Essays on Equality, Law, and Education*, ed. John M. Robson, Toronto: University of Toronto Press, 1984, 85–95.

Carlos Moore, *Pichón: A Memoir: Race and Revolution in Castro's Cuba*, Chicago: Lawrence Hill Books, 2008.

Richard S. Newman, *Freedom's Prophet: Bishop Richard Allen, the AME Church, and the Black Founding Fathers*, New York: New York University Press, 2008.

Nell Irvin Painter, *Sojourner Truth: A Life, a Symbol*, New York: W. W. Norton, 1996.

Kathleen Paul, *Whitewashing Britain: Race and Citizenship in the Postwar Era*, Ithaca: Cornell University, 1997.

Jeffrey B. Perry, *Hubert Harrison: The Voice of Harlem Radicalism, 1883–1918*, New York: Columbia University Press, 2009.

Mike Phillips and Trevor Phillips, *Windrush: The Irresistible Rise of Multi-Racial Britain*, London: HarperCollins, 1998.

Vijay Prashad, *Everybody Was Kung Fu Fighting: Afro-Asian Connections and the Myth of Cultural Purity*, Boston: Beacon Press, 2001.

Paul Rich, *Race and Empire in British Politics*. Cambridge: Cambridge University Press, 1990.

Anthony Sampson, *Mandela: The Authorized Biography*, London: Vintage, 2000.

Joseph A. Soares, *The Decline of Privilege: The Modernization of Oxford University*, Stanford: Stanford University Press, 1999.

Alexis de Tocqueville, *Democracy in America*, ed. Harvey Mansfield and Debra Winthrop, Chicago: University of Chicago Press, 2000.

Mike Wallace, *Between You and Me: A Memoir*, New York: Hyperion, 2005.

INDEX

Note: Page numbers in *italics* refer to illustrations.

disagreements with Malcolm,
39, 134–35
dissolution of relationship
with, 86
influence of, 71
and Kennedy assassination, 25, 40
leadership of, 8
Malcolm's role with, 18
and name of Malcolm, 69, 71–72
relationship with Malcolm, 65
suspension of Malcolm, 25, 32
Muslim Mosque, Incorpo-
rated, 65, 71
Mutualité, Maubert, 153

nationalism, 138–39
Nation of Islam
departure of Malcolm from, 1,
38, 64–65
and name of Malcolm, 71–72
national minister position
in, 25, 32
and Shabazz (term), 69
and speeches of Malcolm, 32
suspension from, 25, 32, 122
threats against Malcolm's life,
65–66
Ndiaye, Pap, 152–53, 157, 158
Negri, Antonio, 125–26
Negritude movement, 27
The New York Times, 40, 44, 93, 94,
98, 156
No Easy Answers (Powell), 106–7
nonviolence principles, 13, 88
Norfolk Penal Colony, 18, 117
Nyobe, Reuben Um, 149

Obama, Barack, 4, 121, 128
The Observer, 54

O'Loughlin, J. L. N., 135
Omi, Michael, 153
"On Repetition in Black Culture"
(Snead), 37
"An Open Letter to Malcolm Little"
(NOI), 71
"Operation Bootstrap," 20
Organization of Afro-American
Unity, 26
Oxford address of Malcolm X,
169–80
audience of, 7, 33, 132, 144
conclusion of, 118
demeanor in, 7, 34, 144
and evolving ideology of Malcolm, 166
"human beings" term in, 84–89
humor in, 57, 76–77, 89, 92, 145
invitation to give, 2
lack of honorarium for, 12–13
and Malcolm's evening interactions, 145–48
memories of, 140–42
perspectives of, 3
photographs from, 11–12,
12, 17, *36*
power as theme of, 31, 95, 118
preparations for, 148
recordings from, 29, 34, 144,
160, 162
relevancy of, 4–5
response to, 118, 144
result of debate, 144
significance of, 3, 33, 132
topic of, 2
"yardstick" reference, 46, 100,
103, 125, 171
Oxford Association of Hotels and
Guest Houses, 19